The
Curse
of the
Boyfriend
Sweater

The

Curse

of the

Boyfriend
Sweater

Essays on Crafting

Alanna Okun

FLATIRON
BOOKS
NEW YORK

www.flatironbooks.com

Designed by Kathryn Parise

Excerpts from "First Rows" and "Knitting Myself Back Together" originally appeared on BuzzFeed.com. Reprinted with permission.

An excerpt from "Homemaking" originally appeared on NPR's *Selected Shorts*.

LIBRARY OF CONGRESS CATALOGING-IN-PUBLICATION DATA

Names: Okun, Alanna, author.
Title: The curse of the boyfriend sweater : essays on crafting / Alanna Okun.
Description: First edition. | New York : Flatiron Books, 2018.
Identifiers: LCCN 2017045150 | ISBN 9781250095619 (hardcover) | ISBN 9781250095626 (ebook)
Subjects: LCSH: Knitting—Anecdotes. | Knitting—Psychological aspects. | Okun, Alanna—Friends and associates. | Knitters (Persons)—United States.
Classification: LCC TT820 .O367 2018 | DDC 746.43/2—dc23
LC record available at https://lccn.loc.gov/2017045150

Our books may be purchased in bulk for promotional, educational, or business use. Please contact your local bookseller or the Macmillan Corporate and Premium Sales Department at 1-800-221-7945, extension 5442, or by email at MacmillanSpecialMarkets@macmillan.com.

First Edition: March 2018

10 9 8 7 6 5 4 3 2 1

To Pat and Pa

CONTENTS

The
Curse
of the
Boyfriend
Sweater

~~~~

Casting On

You can't really know what a project is going to be until it's done. This is true of many things—books, recipes, relationships—and it is especially true of knitting.

Say you want to make a hat. You knit an inch, meant to be the brim, but it's still only the *suggestion* of a brim; a brim isn't a brim until it's attached to a hat. This brim could just as easily become the neck opening for a sweater, if you decide to keep going and have enough yarn. Or you could call it a day and end it right there, making one of those stretchy headbands women in cleanser commercials are always wearing as they splash water on their already-perfect faces. You could decide you still want a hat, but it's going to be ribbed all the way up, or cabled, or a completely different color from the one you started with.

You could plow through the whole project in a single after-noon, the vision of the end product firmly fixed in your mind, or you could set it aside for months at a time, only picking it up to knit a couple of rows when the spirit moves you. You could start it as a gift only to decide you want to keep it for yourself, or the reverse. You could realize it looks nothing like what you intended and either despair or delight. Or, as so often happens, you could reach a place of peaceful ambivalence and decide to just keep pushing through, even though you're not sure, even though you don't know what it will be after you've invested all those hours and all that yarn. You can trust the project to reveal itself to you, outside of your control.

I have always loved control. I like having it, and I also like giving it up in measured doses. This sounds like some sort of BDSM thing, but mostly it plays out for me in my crafting, that interplay of making something just how you want it to be but also allowing for mistakes and detours. I'm a knitter, a crocheter, an embroiderer, and a general dabbler in most fibery pursuits. I've been doing some combination of these things for about as long as I've been on the planet, and they've helped me get through and make sense of some of the hardest-to-control parts of being a person—anxiety, grief, heartbreak, ecstatic joy, total boredom. A craft project allows you to hold something concrete in your hands even when everything around you is swirling and illegible; it allows you to take tiny risks and solve tiny problems and achieve tiny victories. It reminds you that there are calm and good parts of your brain where you can retreat when the rest of it feels like a war zone, and that you can, in some small, brief way, save yourself. Also: you get a lifetime supply of hand-knit socks.

When I talk to people about crafting, nine times out of ten they have never held a needle or spent hours in a yarn store. They don't know about stitch count or care about gauge swatches, the same way I have never really understood what a "fourth down" means. But we usually manage to find some common language, some point of connection where one person or the other goes, "Oh, you too? I thought I was the only one!"[1]

Because I think most people have their version of knitting, or spend their lives trying to find it—that small but constant motion that helps them metabolize the universe and comprises a corner of their identity. For my dad, it's fishing; for my brother, it's music. My mother makes homes and my sister makes art from forgotten objects. Some of my friends draw, some run marathons, some make Internet memes, and some have sat beside me on the couch as they struggle to insert the tip of a needle into a stitch for the first time.

Sometimes, weeks later, I'll get a text message. Usually it's a picture of a ragged but serviceable piece of fabric, inches longer

---

[1] A cribbed version of a favorite quote of mine, attributed to C. S. Lewis; I have an embroidery sampler declaring it next to my front door.

than it had been that first day, the number of holes and mistakes reduced with each newly knitted row.

"Look!" these texts read, in some form or another. "I have no idea what it's going to be, but look!"

I tell them that nobody does, at least not right away. The important thing is to start, even if it's ugly, even if it's hard. Even (especially) if you are the sort of person who is used to having everything exactly the way you want it, who worries that the world will end if one stitch is out of place. The nice thing about the world is that it rarely ends, and even when it does, you can always rip your stitches back and start from the beginning.

First Rows

Anyone who makes things should make something for a baby. There are obvious objections: babies will throw up on the beautiful item you spent months laboring over. They won't appreciate how the slate gray looks next to the mustard yellow, no matter how carefully you selected the yarn. You can't include dainty buttons or tiny pom-poms because babies are super dumb and think everything is food, and, in any case, they'll outgrow whatever it is within weeks. Also: they smell.

But despite all this, there is no better way I can think of to remind yourself that life can come into this world just as it leaves it.

By the time I graduated college, I'd barely ever held a baby, let alone made anything for one of their ilk. They were so foreign and separate from me that I didn't think I'd know where to begin, like trying to make a mitten for a fire hydrant. At my great-grandmother's funeral, my second cousin handed me her infant daughter while she went to the bathroom.[1] The baby's head flopped onto my shoulder and I stood rooted to the spot, petrified that if I moved, I would definitely break her. When her mother came back I was surprised that I missed the weight of that warm, sacklike little body, even if it was filled with spit.

In the following year I made a couple of tiny hats for the newborns of coworkers and choir friends; I started and then abandoned a baby blanket for the family that lived next door to us growing up. (That baby is a sophomore in high school and the blanket is still two rows wide.) But those projects were easy, mindless, no different in construction from scarves or the felted bowls I made to keep laundry quarters in. They didn't require me to narrow or widen my field of vision. And then I found myself knitting a moderately difficult cardigan for a baby who hadn't even been born yet.

I met my best friend, Aude (she introduces herself in one long breath: "Hi-I'm-Aude-like-'Ode-to-Joy'"), the summer after both of us left our respective colleges. I had been living in Poughkeepsie and had never known that thirty minutes away, in a small fairy tale–sounding town called Annandale-on-

---

[1] My great-grandmother died peacefully at ninety-eight, still sharp as ever and in possession of a driver's license.

Hudson, was the girl who would soon make up a fairly large chunk of my everyday life.

We would meet in New York City, where I had moved for the first time and where she had moved back to. Once we met, we would IM throughout the workday and text throughout the night. We would sleep in each other's beds and keep toothbrushes next to each other's sinks. (Aude still refers to hers as "the guest toothbrush," which, ew.) We would meet each other's families: she'd join me at the beach in Rhode Island with my parents on Memorial and Independence and Labor Days, and I would have long, luxurious dinners with her French mother and native New Yorker father at their townhouse in Brooklyn.

During or after one of these dinners, Aude and her mother asked if I would consider a commission: a baby sweater for Aude's godmother's impending child. Despite my misgivings I said yes, of course, anything to help this family that had been so kind to me in my still-new city.

I'd (re)taught Aude to knit in the time we'd known each other, accompanied by a lot of swearing on her part, and the plan was that I would be in charge of the cardigan while she would make a matching hat. In return, her mother would pay for the yarn and Aude would buy me a lot of drinks. It was my first time crafting for anything close to money.

We visited a yarn store a few subway stops away from Aude's parents' house. I'd stayed there with her for a month my first summer in New York and felt as close as I could to familiar in the practically suburban neighborhood, with its detached houses and neat lawns that seemed totally at odds with the rigid, crowded lines of the rest of the city.

Choosing the yarn took time. The baby would be a girl, and we nixed any too-saccharine pastels in favor of a pile of soft gray, with a single ball of cream-colored yarn for the accents: a fluffy pom-pom (too big to fit in any curious mouth) for the hat and lacy edges for the cardigan.

It occurred to me as we left the store that I did not know how to make lacy edges for the cardigan, because I did not know how to make the cardigan. Even though I'd been knitting practically since before I could read, I was used to making things only for myself, or for bodies the size of mine. There were certain indelible rhythms woven into hats and socks, I thought, drummed in by dozens of repetitions. It was too late for me to unlearn them.

Ever the diligent student, I scoured the Internet for the perfect pattern, realizing after I'd bookmarked and saved and doubled back that the one I wanted did not actually exist in a digital format. And so I bought a real, live, physical *book*.

Rightly called *Knitter's Almanac*, it's something of a holy text for knitters; I was semi-ashamed I didn't already own a copy. It's by a woman named Elizabeth Zimmermann, who is widely considered to be the matriarch of modern, unfussy knitting, and even though she has been dead for almost two decades she seemed to understand my anxieties perfectly. Where other patterns specify dimensions and numbers that would have meant nothing to me, she simply wrote, "Don't worry too much about size—babies vary, and knitting stretches."

Still, I doubted at first that the sweater would ever take shape, feared that despite following the recipe I was creating nothing but a monstrous snarl. My sense of scale was entirely thrown off. *How could your head be so large but your shoulders so narrow?* I wondered, working a sleeve too tiny to fit my fist through. *How could a person ever be this small?* I kept thinking I'd have to start over, would have to tell Aude and her mother, *Sorry, it won't be ready in time for the baby shower. How about a gift card from Babies"R"Us instead?*

And yet, after a week or two of knitting on the subway and while waiting for friends at bars, the sweater began to look real. This is one of the benefits of crafting for a tiny human: relatively instant gratification. Before I could visualize what I held in my hands I started to picture the little arms that could fill those sleeves, the chubby belly, the grinning jack-o'-lantern cheeks. It felt like a very small act of hope, especially when the person I was knitting for wasn't even here yet. She was on her way—parties were being thrown and gifts picked out for her arrival—but just out of reach.

I hadn't known that feeling, that anticipation of life, from this direction. I knew its opposite, the feeling of life being ripped suddenly and unfeelingly away. In the year since I'd graduated, two friends had died, both at twenty-two: Marina in a car accident and Jamie of leukemia. The bigness and beginningness of their lives still don't square at all with the fact of their deaths.

I met Marina for the first time twice. Once, during our junior year of college, when we both won a writing contest. She had charged into the awards ceremony with her long hair streaming and her many bracelets clanking.

I thought she was too much. Too noisy, too brash, too everything I secretly wanted to be but instead wrote off with words like "noisy" and "brash." And then the following summer her too-muchness turned out to be exactly the right amount.

I was living in New York for the very first time, subletting a room in a basement apartment and interning at a magazine. On my first day, Marina was the one who happened to pass the glass doors of the office and let me in. I can't remember if she had a feather woven into her hair that day or if it came later, dangling precariously close to her gluten-free soy sauce as we ate roll after roll of sushi in the cafeteria, but I do remember that alert, open look of recognition when she first spotted me. She liked coincidences (there was another intern who, it turned out, had dated my high school boyfriend for years after I did, a topic Marina never got tired of revisiting) and I think she also liked having a buddy, someone to text when she was annoyed or excited by something at work, to talk about love with and what the hell we were going to do when we left school the next year.

I liked having a buddy too. I'd known in some shapeless way that I wanted to be a writer, to live in this world that she and I were visiting for a season, and even though she was my age and hardly had it figured out any more than I did, Marina was the one who made it seem possible. She believed wholeheartedly that we could, even should, lead creative lives and make the things we cared about, that there was great value in writing and performing and feeling out loud and not being afraid to screw it all up and start over. She was just so intensely, irrevocably, unapologetically *herself* that being in her orbit made me better at being me.

I texted her the autumn of our senior year, nine months before the car would hit the guardrail on the highway, about an article she'd just written for her school paper; I'd seen it shared all over Facebook. It was about settling on and settling for careers after graduation—what we'd spent all summer talking about—and I couldn't get it out of my head.

She replied, "We'll obviously be living the same lives forever so I'll see you at our next job."

I met Jamie in college, an hour and a half up the Hudson River from Manhattan. Meeting him at a dorm party our sophomore year was like hearing a new favorite song or casting on stitches for the very first time: *Oh, there you are. I knew someone like you had to exist.*

He didn't write plays or stomp around like Marina; he wrote thoughtful, funny philosophy papers sprinkled with his friends' names ("Suppose Alanna is a brain in a vat . . .") and liked to go for long walks around the campus lake and break into classroom buildings at night. I learned to pick out his sticky-uppy black hair and signature blue hoodie in any crowd. His voice was so quiet and low that you sometimes had to lean in to hear him.

He lived two houses down from me our senior year and then across Prospect Park when we both moved to Brooklyn after graduation. We weren't really in each other's worlds but I loved to visit his and invite him into mine, where we would drink tea and beer, and play increasingly sloppy rounds of Bananagrams. He'd grill anything he could get his hands on (veggie burgers, portobello mushrooms, grapefruit) and douse it all in this sticky-sweet barbecue sauce called Sweet Baby Ray's. I keep a bottle in my fridge all the time now. In our last semester at school, when he was in remission, he'd ask in that half-joking way friends of knitters do when I was going to make him something. I would laugh and say that I'd make him a long stocking cap or a tent for the yard we shared, and never did.

Maybe my favorite kiss ever was my first (of only a handful, because that wasn't really what it was about) with Jamie. We were standing outside a party at the beginning of junior year, on one of those nights you know might be the last real warm one of summer, talking with other people but always keeping the other in arm's reach. Somewhere around midnight, we left together.

"Want to try to get into Rocky?" he asked me. Rockefeller Hall was the imposing classroom building plopped in the middle of campus. I was always afraid of getting in trouble but I would have gone anywhere with him just then, so I said yes.

We orbited the outside, looking for a window that had been left open, and found one just as we were about to give up and go home. I followed him up the stairs to the top floor and down the narrow hall lined with professors' offices. I can't remember now if the lights were on—maybe just the Exit sign? Maybe the glow of our phones?—but somehow Jamie found this tiny door, about half the size of a normal one, outside the women's bathroom. I must have passed it twenty times over my time at school and never noticed. He was like that: he made you notice.

He jiggled it open to reveal a crawl space, probably meant for storage, and crawled into the blackness. And I, scared of the dark and of small spaces and of anything I couldn't see, went with him. He shut the door behind me.

I've gone back to that memory so many times it's starting to fray. Those small, suspended moments when the person you've wanted looks at you, sees you, even in the dark wants you right back—I would grab them by the fistful and spin them into fiber if I could, knit them up into a blanket and burrow forever into its folds.

Jamie would go on to be in love with someone else and so would I, a few times. I would always want him in a way that he did not want me, but instead of letting that repel him, he would take it and remake it into a firm and constant friendship. He would go to London the following semester and come back early to receive his diagnosis, would take the summer and the fall to get treatment, to get so skinny and pale that when I saw him one day visiting campus it was like seeing his ghost; he would return to school in remission and finish on time with the rest of us, would give me advice on love and writing, would move to the city in the summer, would slip back into sickness when it got colder, would die on one of the first warm days of spring. All of it, and still I clutch that one memory, that single stitch in time.

For months after Marina and then Jamie died, I saw them all over the city. I'd catch a glimpse of her sharp nose or his spiky hair and then I'd realize that of course it wasn't her, there was no way it could be him. That absence felt like missing a stair, like choking on a gulp of water gone down the wrong part of my throat.

Now the missing is more abstract. Because they died so young, because my time with them both was so short, I wore out my few memories a long time ago. And so I transpose the two of them into places they never actually were. I think of Jamie when I play games, all types, even ones we didn't play together and I'm not sure he ever had the chance to learn. Would he have liked cribbage or Settlers of Catan, or found them tedious? I imagine him at the parties I go to, populated by people we went to college with, and wonder if even now his RSVP on Facebook would make sure that I got there too, even on tired Fridays when Greenpoint or the Upper East Side is too far to contemplate. I walk through his old neighborhood and think about what it would be like to text him for a drink, to play a round of Scrabble, to hug him goodbye and catch the once-familiar, now-forgotten smell of the back of his neck.

Marina I picture at work, and on Twitter, and at different parties from the Jamie ones. Book parties, theatre parties, parties where people stand around and yell above the music about how underpaid and overqualified they are, where they ask how one another's art and love lives are going and later dump the replies into a strainer to find the nugget of truth, the reassurance that they themselves are doing all right by comparison. Would she and I have stayed friends, or would it have become one of those acquaintanceships where the only thing we had to talk about was the fact that we met at such a heightened, specific time?

"Did you know we interned together?" we'd tell our friends the first few times we crossed paths, before fading into smiles and waves and the occasional counting of bylines.

I don't know what they would be to me now. All I know is that I am now older than either of them will ever be, and that scares me. The loss of those two people took up so much space that when I was asked to knit the baby sweater, six months after Jamie's death and a little over a year after Marina's, I had all but forgotten about the idea of new life.

Making it was a tangible reminder. Making anything feels like seizing control, like defiant reversal in the face of grief: this thing is yours, the way you would like it to be, and it exists where before there was nothing. And with each row you knit on something meant for a baby, you start to see his or her outlines more clearly, waiting to be fully formed. I liked knowing that the sweater-to-be was in my bag during the workday and by my bed when I woke up. I felt it glow; I felt it breathe.

I finished with a few days to spare. Aude suggested that I sew a little tag with my initials into the sweater before handing it over.

"Who knows," she said. "Maybe it'll become an heirloom or something." She said that whoever got it next—after this baby, who would be named Maya, who could turn out loud and present like Marina or quiet and kind like Jamie or endlessly open like Aude—would want to know where it came from.

A few weeks after I handed over the cardigan, Aude sent me some pictures. They were of the new parents and Maya, born the night before. The baby looked tiny and quizzical, with a shock of black hair that would have made bald infant-me insanely jealous. She was still too small to fit the sweater, or even the matching hat that Aude had started and that I had wound up finishing. (We had always known that would happen.)

That, I thought, was good. It gave her something to grow into.

Not Just for Grandmas

~~~~~~

I f I read one more article that begins with a line like "Knitting: it's not just for grandmas anymore!" I'm ripping it up
with a felting needle.

Variations on this sentence are everywhere, peppering trend
pieces about how millennials are flocking to the fiber arts and
leading breathless news items about how knitting adds twenty
years to your life and burns more calories than doing yoga while
having sex.[1] And look: I'm glad people are writing about the
love of my life. I'm just not happy with the language they all
too often use to describe it.

Not Just for Grandmas™ reduces knitting (and crafting as

---

[1] Please read every time I type "millennial," of which this will hopefully be the last,
with as many ironic tildes and asterisks and quotation marks as you can fit in your
field of vision. Actually, one more mention: here I primarily mean millennial *women*.
When men are spotted crafting in the wild, it's worth its very own stand-alone article.

a whole) to a cultural punch line, trotted out as a mild but harmless anachronism. Young people! Using their hands! Not even for sexting on their iWhatevers or dismantling the economy! Those millennials, always up to something quirky and inefficient.[2] It's the thinking that's at work when lady characters in rom-coms or sitcoms or any-other-coms are depicted cradling a pair of knitting needles and a bottle of wine (plus maybe a cat or two for good measure) when they don't have anything better to do on a Saturday night: knitting is so backward and boring that of course you only do it when you're not equipped to face the real world.

A smaller but related pet peeve of mine is when knitting is incorrectly depicted in movies or on TV. Someone clacks two sticks against each other and a sock appears, or the yarn is held nowhere near the tips of the needles. There used to be a blog cataloging these mistakes—thatsnothowyouknit.tumblr.com—and while it might seem pedantic, just think of how much time and money go into producing even a second of screen time. Think of all the takes, all the rewrites, all the costumes and the salaries and the sets. Or, in the case of animation, all the hundreds of hours spent making sure every detail is consistent. And nobody could be called in to confirm whether a character is holding the yarn correctly? Actually, I would love to be a freelance knitting consultant, so if you are the head of a major studio please hit me up.

---

2 Last one, truly, in the whole entire book.

I'm sure the authors of these articles and creators of these shows don't set out to be dismissive; they (or their editors) probably think they're being clever and original, or they're not thinking at all. It's not their world and so they fall back on shorthand to describe it—I've absolutely been guilty of that in my own writing. When Pinterest first came onto the scene it was treated to the same kind of lazy introduction: wasn't it novel and funny that a glorified Internet scrapbook, with its *recipes* and *clothes* and *houses*, had real value? That someone (a lot of someones) had poured actual advertising dollars into such a service?

But these "soft" things do matter. What we put in and on and around our bodies is important, and so are the things we create. They're a series of choices we get to make when we may not be able to choose much else: our jobs, our loves and losses, our place in the world. And so maybe in some accidental way, those sad-sack sitcom jokes about knitting contain a grain of truth: making things can certainly help you navigate when the outside world gets to be too much. The difference is, we've chosen to do it.

Taken one at a time, these slights are petty annoyances; together, they paint an ugly, sexist picture. Crafters are told that we have to have permission to indulge in our pursuits, bestowed by the *Whatever Tribune* or blahdiblah.com, because otherwise all we should be is embarrassed by them. That's tacitly what these types of clunky, thoughtless trend pieces do: assume a beginning and an endpoint. They deny roots and they erase nuance, variance, and the lives of actual, real-life people who have spent their passion and energy learning how to create the world they want.

Which leads us to my least favorite part of Not Just for Grandmas™: how disrespectful it is to the grandmas! Grandmas rule! I can't wait to be one! So many people's stories about crafting begin with a grandmother, my own included, and that should be a point of pride, not disavowal.

"I was six/twelve/thirty when my grandma decided it was time for me to knit/crochet/embroider," these stories begin, recounted to new acquaintances at yarn stores, to strangers on subways, or to old friends at bars. Often they're offered as answers to questions: "What are you doing?" "When did you start?" "Why do you always carry around so many needles?"

Sometimes the grandmother in question is stern and withholding, only giving the storyteller rare flashes of affection when he or she struggles to knit a first crooked row. Sometimes the grandmother is kindly, forever pausing crochet lessons to pull another sheet of sugar cookies from the oven. Sometimes she is on her deathbed, intent on passing down a skill before she goes, and sometimes she lives long enough to stitch bibs for every one of the storyteller's children.

Often the grandmother is not a grandmother at all, but a middle school teacher, or a church group, or an uncle. Sometimes the grandmother is your age or much younger. Sometimes the grandmother is YouTube. The fact remains that knitting and its cousins aren't innate skills. They're taught and they're learned and reinforced and passed down, in an interlocking series of loops that builds and layers just like the crafts themselves. Why should we feel flattered when some news outlet tells us not to worry, we're so much *cooler* and *hotter* and *more modern* than the people who were once so generous with us?

Look, I'm being 1,000,000 percent defensive here. I know there are much, much bigger cultural battles to wage, and that no matter how clumsily some of these articles are written, at least one of them resulted in at least one person visiting a craft store for the first time. That makes it all worthwhile. But the sanctity and value of making things feels like it's worth defending, and when you're armed with pointy sticks, it's that much easier to stab back.

My own grandmother—my mother's mother—made blankets. Afghans, she called them, a word I liked to repeat over and over on our visits to her house in Virginia, when I was still small enough to wrap myself up in one like an orange-and-purple burrito. They were a riot of dignified jewel tones that matched the colors in her outfits, her home, and her jewelry. (She never pierced her ears and so wore large, beautiful clip-ons her whole life. I still pause to look at the clip-on selection whenever I'm in a jewelry store, even though my ears have been pierced since I was thirteen.) She crocheted the afghans while watching TV with my grandpa, and I don't know how many she made in total but it felt like many dozens, hundreds of hours of flashing hooks darting in and out of an ever-growing heap of nubbly fabric.

I loved to watch her. I liked it the way some people like watching Olympic skiing even when they themselves have never set foot on a mountain: the speed of it, the almost superhuman elegance, that entirely new but somehow familiar method of moving through the world. I liked how she had complete control over whatever it was she happened to be creating, and how for every cause (that flicky gesture I couldn't imitate no matter how long I stared) there was a direct effect (a stitch!). I liked to watch the pile of crocheted squares mount next to my grandma's armchair, and I especially liked when I would come back six months or a year later to find that the squares had become, somehow, a blanket.

My first project was a blanket too, although not one large enough for even the tiniest human. It was a rectangular piece of light-turquoise fabric, knitted under the supervision of my grandma one weekend at the beach. My family—my parents, my little sister, my little brother, and I, plus my mom's folks and her sister, Kathleen—would go every year to a rented house in Delaware. The same way the word "afghan" stuck in my head, so too did the idea that going to the beach in Delaware was somehow very funny. Who knew there were beaches in *Delaware*? Weren't all the beaches supposed to be in Florida, or maybe Cape Cod?

Still, even as a know-it-all brat I loved the house we returned to, with its high, swooping ceilings and seashell-encrusted knickknacks. I even enjoyed the twelve hours it took to drive there from Massachusetts. My mom would pile us into the little blue Subaru in which I would, a decade and two attempts later, get my driver's license. Moriah (my sister) and Matthew (my brother) and I would listen to *The Chronicles of Narnia* and Harry Potter audiobooks on the cassette player and fall asleep on one another's shoulders, waking up when we stopped at a Hampton Inn in New Jersey. It was our designated halfway point and always struck me as extremely glamorous, mostly because of the breakfast buffet.

My memories from the beach town—Fenwick Island—have melted together into a swirl of boardwalk visits and shell-collecting expeditions. I, the oldest and the bossiest, directed these journeys, gamely followed by my grandma with her metal detector, the others bringing up the rear. I do not know where those shells are now but I do have three distinct memories I carry around:

I am seven or eight, embroiled in a down-to-the-wire game of Pictionary Junior. It's our family's game of choice and nobody is given any slack, no matter how young or old. I am extremely competitive even though I am not that good at games or sports (a fact that persists until the present and feels like a minor curse). But I win this round by guessing, with hardly a doodle of a square to go off of, that the clue in question is, in fact, "Pictionary." It is my first exposure to the concept of "meta" and I am very pleased with myself.

A few years later my characteristically gentle grandfather sneaks up behind me outside the haunted house at the boardwalk. His coat is lifted over his head and he grabs me. I am so scared I cry. He feels terrible and takes me back to the haunted house a few days later, shows me that I have nothing to be afraid of. (The paint is peeling and you can see the bolts.) I tell this story at his funeral and people laugh, because he had been so thoughtful, so caring, so every inch the inquisitive and nurturing college professor that it's like saying I'd caught Santa Claus smoking a cigarette.

And the year I am six, when it rains. In fact, it hurricanes—the storm is called Floyd, which is much too dorky a moniker for a disaster that causes the boardwalk to be shuttered and all seashell endeavors to be postponed indefinitely. Matthew has not yet been born (he'll come along in February) and I am bored of Moriah, who is three, after all the days spent cooped up inside together. I am whiny enough that my grandma pulls me up on the couch beside her and gives me a pair of dark-blue aluminum knitting needles. I keep them forever.

She shows me how to get the first stitches onto the needle. She shows me how to hold the yarn (behind the tip), how to make a stitch (over, around, and through), and how to let the old stitch drop (carefully, steadily, trusting that it will all be okay). She tells me not to tug too hard or the stitches will turn out too tight, and patiently helps me work my way through the next far-too-tight row when I do not listen. I'm frustrated, at first—I'm always frustrated when I can't pick something up right away, whether it's Pictionary or cursive—but soon I'm working the rows myself, without my grandma's fingers on my own to guide them. It starts to feel less like tripping over my feet and more like swimming in the ocean, and then like pulling into the driveway at the end of a long trip.

We sit there for I don't know how long, but I do know that at the end, when my grandma shows me how to finish the piece by casting off, I have this . . . thing. It's not a scarf or a hot pad, too stubby and small to be much of anything, but it is very definitely an object. Someone, I think Aunt Kathleen, suggests that it could be a blanket for a stuffed animal, and that's as good a purpose as any.

Over subsequent visits to Fenwick Island and to her house in Virginia, my grandma shows me new techniques: how to purl, how to knit in the round. It opens me up to the bottomless world of hats, sleeves, mittens, and, one day in the far-off future, socks. I am at first too impatient to learn how to read patterns so I improvise, feeling my way through hats and scarves until they become a little less uneven, a little less lumpy, a little more shaped the way human bodies are supposed to be.

Soon I move beyond my grandmother's couch and start to learn from a handful of knitting books and a constellation of websites. I grudgingly learn how to decipher patterns and soon I can't remember what it's like not to be able to, the way you don't quite know what it was like before you knew how to read. I even make up a move or two. I get better, I lose interest, I regain it, I improve. I get a boyfriend, I get into college, I get a job, I knit. I am anxious, I am joyful, I am lonely, I knit.

I haven't stopped knitting, really, since that day at the beach. I've steadily amassed more needles and more yarn, in all sizes, in all colors. It suits my tendency to collect things—the seashells, the dollhouse miniatures I liked to arrange as a child in what I called "setups" despite the fact that I never actually cared about dolls. Periodically, I would lay out all the fiber on the floor of my room, like some unibrowed little bird in her rainbow nest. Now I keep it in a bookshelf in the apartment where I live by myself, still organized by color. It's the same idea: I like surrounding myself with the possibility of it, the reminder that whenever I want or need to, I can grab a ball and start to make something new. I get to be both bigger than myself and exactly the right size.

I've wondered if that's how it feels for everyone, when and if you find your thing. Not necessarily your calling, not exactly your passion, not a pursuit that you hope will bring you money or glory or a sense of elevation to a higher plane. Not even something that takes up a lot of space, but fits into your life so seamlessly it's like there was always room for it. Just that quiet "ahh" of slipping into place, of a running shoe slapping the pavement, of the harmony found in a choir. Of a stitch sliding from one needle to the next.

I never got the chance to ask my grandma if that's what

knitting—or crocheting or saxophone playing or singing or gardening or one of the dozens of ways she built a life—felt like for her. No, that's not true—I had plenty of chances. I had twenty-five years of couches and Christmases. I just never thought to ask.

Because unlike apocryphal grandmothers, Patricia Furey (Pat, or Ma, or Mama) didn't just make blankets. She made music in her town band and choir, and she made sure that my mom, Kathleen, and their brother (named Michael, like my grandpa) had music in their bones too. She graduated high school when she was fifteen and got her master's in sociology in her forties. She coaxed plants from dirt with the same magic she worked on sticks and string, and she loved us all fiercely, if at times a little critically. (My overplucked eyebrows were forever a sticking point, as was the unnatural purply red I dyed my hair back in high school. I willfully ignored her advice and now, with brows that have grown in and bad dye that has grown out, realize I've followed it to the letter.) She demanded the most comfortable, the most quiet, and the least drafty seats in restaurants even when the rest of us cringed behind her. She hosted Christmas in her living room every year. She wanted us to be our best.

"No one loves me like she does," my mother said to me on the phone a few days before her mother died, when we were already halfway to knowing that's what would happen. I wanted to say that I loved her, that I could learn to love her even bigger to make up for whatever loss was coming, but I knew that wasn't it. Later, with the person who knitted the first row of everything I would ever make in my life now gone, I dimly started to know what my mother meant.

What happens to an object when its creator is gone? It's hard to know what tense to use when describing my grandma's many projects. The blankets still exist—they *are* orange, it feels wrong to say that they *were* orange—but they've undergone a phase change. They weigh more and yet take up less space because there will be no more of them. There will be no more arguments in restaurants and no more enveloping hugs. And what happens to an object when it's been given and then returned? I knitted my grandma so many things, first very bad and then pretty good. The Christmas before she died, I made her socks, which my mother gave back to me after the funeral. It wasn't the wrong thing to do—even worse would be for them to get lost, to be loved and used by no one—but I can't bring myself to wear them, although I doubt my grandma ever did. They look empty even though socks are supposed to be empty.

Missed Connections

You: Girl on Manhattan-bound F train, knitting what looked like a sock—didn't get a good look because you disembarked one stop after I got on.

Me: Girl who wished I had my own knitting on hand so I could pull it out in solidarity, or at least that there were some kind of secret hand signal to indicate that I'm one of you, and not just some creep staring at you from across the car.

You: Hot guy knitting on the L train.

Me: Someone who never actually saw you, but who received two text messages from two separate friends on the same day informing me that they'd found my soul mate. Unless you're two different dudes, in which case, hello to both of you.

You: Lady who seemed scandalized by my embroidery on the N train.

Me: Sorry for stitching the phrase "Butt Stuff" in public. In my defense, it was for a friend.

You: Entire ridership of that one car on the M.

Me: Grateful that none of you laughed when I attempted to knit while standing up, even when I dropped my ball of yarn and it rolled under a nearby seat.

You: Woman whom I spoke to for a long time on the 7, the first summer I lived in New York. You were a few years older than me and very pretty, with hair pulled back in one of those ponytails where you wrap a piece of hair around the elastic so it looks super fancy and deliberate. When you saw I was knitting you sat down next to me and spent the entire ride into Queens telling me about your own crafts, your favorite yarn stores, and your plans to start selling your stuff. You gave me your number—it's still in my phone as "Christina Knitting"—and made me feel like the world was just the right kind of expansive.

Me: Sorry I never had the courage to text.

You: Manspreaders.

Me: Crusader in the fight for personal space, who uses her knitting as a cover for jostling the elbows of people who take up far more than their fair and reasonable share of the subway bench.

You: Older woman on the Delancey J platform crocheting faster than I can blink.

Me: Fake redhead who wants to learn your witchery.

You: Extremely kind pair of German tourists on the Brooklyn-bound G.

Me: Sobbing girl to whom you gave a bunch of tissues and an Andes mint. Jamie had died a few weeks before and I'd thought I was done with the sneak attacks of grief, but I guess I wasn't. One of you told me, "Whatever it is, it'll be okay." At the time, this didn't feel applicable to my situation, but now I think you were right. This isn't about knitting or anything but I've regarded Andes mints with great affection ever since.

You: Beautiful braided scarf I knitted from soft gray merino yarn that cost way more than I will ever admit.

Me: Idiot who left you on some train one night when I was drunk.

You: Whoever picked up the braided scarf.

Me: Its maker, who sincerely hopes that you love it.

You: Guy on the R who told me my knitting reminded you of your grandmother, and then asked for my number.

Me: Uninterested woman who hopes, for your own good and the good of ladykind, that you never try a line like that again.

The Curse of the
Boyfriend Sweater

W̲e broke up before I'd even bought the yarn.

       I'd knitted Sam[1] a lot of things in the years we'd known each other: a beanie he could wear to work, a cowl to keep his neck warm while he biked around Brooklyn, a pair of gray socks with red heels that were the exact inverse of a pair I'd made myself. Once I'd tried to knit him a bow tie, a spectacularly floppy failure that we laughed about together when he unwrapped it. The one thing I hadn't made him was a sweater, and so that—large, gray, and cozy—would be his Christmas present.

       But there was the small matter of the curse. Every knitter (and most crocheters) knows about the Curse of the Boyfriend Sweater. It's essentially the opposite of Engagement Chicken,

---

[1] That's not his real name.

guaranteeing that if you set out to knit your partner a sweater, the relationship will end before you've finished.[2] I had read hushed horror stories and equally staunch dismissals in the knitting magazines and all over the sites I frequented. I believed in it the way I believe losing my keys is caused by Mercury in retrograde or that I'm bossy because I'm an Aries: a not-quite-tongue-in-cheek explanation, a convenient way of keeping things in order. Part of the lore of my people, maybe, but not something to seriously take to heart.

Sam was not the first boy I knitted for; before him, I'd spent most of a decade in a series of back-to-back relationships. Ever since I can remember, I've thought of myself as a girlfriend. I'm good at it. I like the daily routine of goodnight texts and bleary-eyed morning sex, paying each other back for takeout and bus tickets, proofreading each other's cover letters and getting to know each other's friends. I like standing around at a party with one thumb hooked through the other's belt loop, and squabbling over which movie showing we'll reasonably be able to catch, and realizing halfway through a fight that the real fight isn't about the thing you're fighting about at all. I like to be able to look back and say, *Hey, look at this life we've*

---

[2] For the blessedly unaware, Engagement Chicken is a recipe mythologized in the annals of women's magazines, ensuring that your man (always styled thusly) will propose by the end of the meal if you (always a woman) prepare it for him.

built. Like knitting a scarf or a sweater and watching the stitches pile up row by row: there goes a month, there goes a year. You can wrap yourself in the knowledge that someone has chosen you, someone sees you, and in that way, you are safe.

There is, of course, the other side. When I'm not with somebody I can get destabilized, a little manic, straining against the edges of my life like I'm trying to squeeze my head through a neck hole that's too small. *On to the next one*, that mean voice inside me hisses, *unless you've used it all up, unless you're no longer worth it, unless all those times before were just a fluke.* Being in a relationship is a Band-Aid of reassurance that no matter how flawed and fearful I may be, I'm still doing something right. That there is always someone there who will save me even if I can't save myself. And so I've grabbed for it with both hands without pausing to ask if it's what I really want.

For almost all of my boyfriends, I crafted. If you hang around me long enough, odds are good that I will try to drape you in yarn—over winter break of my senior year of college I made two sweaters, an infinity scarf, and a pair of cashmere socks for my four housemates, because I loved them dearly but also because I'd run out of parts of my own body to decorate. I make Christmas presents for my family nearly every year, and after that first baby sweater came a series of tiny hats one month after the other, as if everyone I knew had gotten together and drawn up a birthing schedule.

But with the boyfriends, it went beyond simple proximity. There is so much tied up in a handmade gift, so much that it can feel like a miniature version of the relationship itself. What do they want? (Cowl, hat, gloves.) Is it really what they want at all? (Three pairs of abandoned gloves on the top shelf of the hall closet, never remembered when needed.) What are you willing to give? (Cashmere is so expensive but so warm.) Or learn? (Who knew glove needles were so fiddly to use?) Do you know their body as well as you think you do? (Hands the size of catcher's mitts, really should have stuck with the piano.)

Will you hide it while you're working on it, only wanting your partner to see the finished product? Will you save it for a special event—a birthday, an anniversary—or present it when it's needed, that first morning when they look out the window and groan about steering their bike through all that snow? Are you waiting for a specific response when you do hand it over—"It's perfect." "You're perfect." "I love you and how could I ever leave?"

Because your gift is an assertion. "*I love you,*" it says. "I love you times ten thousand stitches and fourteen consecutive subway rides. I love you enough to keep you warm, and I love you enough to know what you need and therefore who you are, and in exchange I want you to think of me and want me and feel me there even when I am not with you." It's not a selfless act; a handmade object can serve almost like a walkie-talkie, a piece of string between two cups that the maker can whisper through: "I was here. I matter."

The first boy I knitted for was also named Sam.[3] We met at performing arts camp, and I loved him in the slack-jawed way that only a recently bat mitzvahed theatre geek can. I spent the summer staring at this wiry boy who wore his hair in carefully maintained spikes, laughing at his improv performances and listening to at least three of my friends talk about how much they liked him too. I was surprised when he asked for my AIM screen name at the end of the summer, asked me to take a walk around the town center, asked me if he could kiss me on the overstuffed armchair in my bedroom.

Our braces clinked and I was so happy I didn't know where to put it all. I had planned my outfit so carefully that I remember it now, half a lifetime later, but I hadn't planned for this rush, this feeling of arrival.[4] I hadn't known until then that liking someone meant they could maybe like you back.

Sam 1.0 and I dated for six months, a lifetime by eighth-grade standards. He lived one town away and our parents had to drive us to all our dates. We made out at the movies and in our darkened living rooms. He once took me out to dinner and

---

[3] Also not his real name.

[4] A light-blue cropped hoodie from Delia*s over a purple camisole, which at the time was referred to as a "cami."

paid with a $50 bill, which I found incredibly suave. I met his family and his friends and was thrilled when it seemed that they genuinely liked me, didn't think it was odd that this golden, glowing person would want me in his life. I remember his older sister leaving to go back to college after a break and telling me, "Take care of my brother," which seemed such a solemn and grown-up promise to make in a flurry of goodbye hugs. I'd been given a cell phone the previous year when I'd started walking home from school and spoke to Sam on it in between our reams of AIM conversations. (Measured in reams because of course I printed them all out.)

He told me he loved me for the first time over that phone. I started to knit him a scarf with green yarn. I didn't think about us ending because I had no conception that we *could* end; I loved him and he loved me, so that was how things were now.

Just like I hadn't known what it was to be loved, I also hadn't known that the other person was allowed to stop loving you. And then one night at his house he told me that he was sorry, but he wanted to break up. I felt not so much sadness just then as shock—those weren't the rules. He was supposed to be on my team, be my person, not just decide to leave one day without giving me a chance to make it right. What was I supposed to do with all of these feelings, all this time, all this space in myself I'd set aside for him? How could I go back to being just me?

It remains one of the kindest breakups I've ever been a part of. My mom couldn't come back to pick me up for another couple of hours, or maybe I just didn't want to tell her what had happened over the phone, so Sam and I watched *L.A. Confidential* and he let me cry into his neck. I spent the rest of the school year crying, and the following summer at camp I met a different boy, and then another the summer after that. I never finished the green scarf I'd started for Sam; eventually I unraveled it and used the yarn to make a lumpy, experimental pair of slippers, which I never wore.

I made more scarves and a couple of hats for the camp boyfriends, for a guy a few years ahead of me in high school, for the tall bassist who came over to talk to me one day in the town library and turned out to be the boy I'd date for the next two years. Joe asked to borrow my AP US History textbook and I only found out after we'd been together for months that he was taking Modern African History at his all-boys Catholic school down the road.

He drove us around in the old white Volvo he'd christened "White Heat" and took pictures of everything, me and my sister and all of our friends, turned the flatness of our suburban town into something layered and exciting. Sometimes we smoked weed and once my mom found a teal Trojan wrapper on the floor of my bedroom. Mostly, though, we were content to listen to music and play video games and lie with our heads on each other's stomachs. This is what it is, I'd think, looking at him and the hundreds of photographs he'd logged of our time together, to have a partner, a buddy, a witness. He made me feel so seen.

I tried to make him socks the summer after we graduated from our respective high schools, when I was anxious and unemployed and had plenty of time to learn knitting techniques. They did not turn out well, more like the universe's most depressing Christmas stockings than anything meant for a human foot.[5] And then summer was over, and I was leaving for school in upstate New York, and he would be staying in Boston. I was restless and impatient, in such a hurry to get where I was headed next that I think now I was unkind, didn't listen with more than half an ear when he told me that he'd miss me, that he wanted to visit, that we should try to make it work.

"Maybe you're allergic to peaches," my freshman roommate offered on the second night of college as I dry-heaved over our trash can.

Maybe, I thought, or maybe I'd had one too many PBRs, but the nausea turned out to be a panic attack, the first of many I would have in the following years. That night it came on because I felt violently lonely and constricted by that loneliness, and my body didn't know how to process it. It was about Joe, to a point, but larger and more shapeless than any absence was this sense that I had been a girlfriend for so long and all of a

---

[5] In fact, they might well have begun as socks for me before I realized they'd be much too large to fit any feet smaller than Joe's size 16s. He has since—no lie—gone on to model XXL socks in a print ad for American Apparel.

sudden wasn't anymore. I had done this to myself; I was the thing that was broken.

I didn't feel that way for long. Instead, I outran it. Two months later I came as close as I ever had to challenging the curse by crocheting a sweater for my new college boyfriend. He was a tall, skinny sophomore with curly black hair and bright-blue eyes, and even though his name was Michael, nobody called him that unless they were making fun of him. Instead, he went by Hirschey, a spin on his last name. I liked how it turned my mouth into a smile whenever I said it.

I'd met him the first week of classes and immediately we'd fallen into each other, spending every night in his tiny, clothes-strewn single room two floors away from mine. Each Sunday we'd order a large square pizza from the drunk-food place across the street and we'd nibble on it throughout the week; sometimes we'd supplement with boxes of Cheez-Its and glazed doughnut holes. We were so excited by the freedom, so excited to *be* excited by each other. I thought about Joe and my home-town and my high school sometimes, but it was just easier to look ahead than to stop and sort through what I'd left behind.

The sweater was a monstrously heavy garment made from black acrylic yarn during a semester's worth of art history lec-tures; my hook ducked and wove through Caravaggio, Kahlo, and Koons. Hirschey wore it gamely through a few Hudson Valley winters, even accompanied me to a yarn festival, where I trotted him around like a living mannequin. When we finally decided to end things after two and a half years, hundreds of nights, infinite pizzas, it felt like it was time. I hardly knew college without him; we were both ready for something different.

After a period of not speaking, we started a ritual on Sundays. He'd pick me up in his roommate's car and we'd drive to a legendarily weird twenty-four-hour diner near campus decorated with neon pictures of Greek ruins. We'd split gravy-covered disco fries and milkshakes and fill each other in on our weeks. We'd eventually talk about the people we were falling for and the ones who bruised our hearts. And then he graduated, and by then, I wasn't sad to see the sweater go.

What started to worry me wasn't the near-relentless pace of my dating life. It was the edges I smoothed away with my blinding desire to get to the next place, the next person, to tell a compact story. "Serial monogamist!" said with a smile and a wink is an easy way to avoid talking about the hurt I've received (and doled out) in ever-shifting measures. It implies an ease, an effortlessness, skipping from rock to rock without ever stumbling.

It elides the boys whose heels I nipped at for months before they turned toward other girls or just away from me; it erases the headachey mornings spent stumbling back to my own bed, not floaty with hope but heavy, laden. So many people I slotted into the boyfriend space because they were there, only to realize much later that they didn't fit or didn't want to fit. So many times I cried furiously at myself for not being enough. And I've done it too, more times than probably even I know: hardened and retreated in that exact way I so dread from others. I've had next boyfriends fixed in my sights before the old ones were gone because I couldn't imagine confronting a gap, a moment of silence, of stillness.

And then there was Sam. We met in college, where he was a year ahead of me. I'd watched him perform in a musical and liked him instantly: his high cheekbones and cute, slim butt and laugh like a sexy jackhammer. (He remains one of the only people I could ever sit in a theater with and not feel self-conscious about my own choking-sea-lion laugh.) We spent months eyeing each other at parties and making fun of each other after a cappella concerts and then two weeks before he graduated, one of us left a bar near campus and the other followed.[6] Ten days later I left his house and cried all the way back to Boston.

I'd thought that would be the end of it. He'd written me a letter on a thank-you note from the college bookstore ("I'm sorry for the inappropriateness of my stationery," it began, "but it was all they had") and then, I figured, he'd be gone, absorbed into adult life while I stayed behind and finished my last year of school.

That summer I sublet a basement room on the Upper East

---

[6] Probably everyone should have made fun of us after a cappella concerts.

Side. Sam stayed on campus to work at a theatre program. We were living at either end of the Metro-North Hudson train line, and one weekend not long after I arrived in New York, he took the train down to my borrowed bedroom. A few weeks later, I took it back up to his dorm-issued twin bed. Without ever really talking about it, that became our rhythm. (I went back to school not long ago and could barely fit my own self into one of those beds; I'm no larger now than I was then but I guess I take up more space. It must have taken some ship-in-a-bottle physics to get us both into one together.)

Sam was New York City for me in the way that first basement sublet was, that first temporary job alongside Marina. The way Joe was my hometown and Hirschey was college. Sam bounded around the city with his endless energy and long limbs, taking me to strange off-off-off-Broadway plays and dinners we could afford with our collectively zero money. Something in me lit up whenever I got a text that he was coming my way, or an invitation to a show and a sleepover back upstate. He added a hazy excitement to that time, which must have been made, at least in part, of the fact that I was never totally sure he'd be coming back.

And then, again, that intoxicating feeling of being seen. The way he studied me and asked me questions made me feel like this life I was starting to build was important, like my day-to-day choices—what I made for breakfast, the way I sat when I read, what I thought about people and plays and dry martinis—had meaning and weight, weren't just the result of a series of subconscious accidents like I sometimes suspected. I hardly wrote or crafted at all that summer, telling myself I was too busy with work and with the city and with him; really I think it was that I felt too heightened to make much of anything, too fragile, too worried that if I looked away or inward even for a minute, it would all disappear.

We switched places in the fall—Sam moved to Brooklyn and I went back to Poughkeepsie for my last year of college—and dissolved. It was a relief, really, to have myself back in one place again. But I never shook that singular, staticky feel of him. We kept in half-touch, dated other people. I spent senior year without a boyfriend, for once. I tried out for the first play I'd been in since high school (*The Vagina Monologues*, obviously) and wrote my thesis and soaked up my last months at this place that had loved me so well. I made out with roughly half the school. I graduated. I moved to New York City, just like everybody else. I met Aude and started my job. I started to make things again.

Sam sent me a message on my twenty-third birthday, a few days after Jamie died. He knew—our school was small. We chatted a little and discovered that we didn't live very far from each other, and so decided to meet for brunch early one afternoon.

Oh, I thought as I walked up and there he was, tall in a red-and-white-checked shirt, glasses thicker and rounder than they'd been in college, dark, wavy hair as shiny as ever. Like an actor playing the fuzzy version of him that had been living in my memory. *Right. That's what I've been missing.*

After that we met for a show, and then for a midday movie with a smuggled Nalgene bottle full of Manhattans (water never tasted the same from it after that, no matter how many times he rinsed it out). I didn't let him kiss me for weeks because I knew what it would do to me. I'd be sent right back to that place of waiting for his messages, waiting to be wanted the way I wanted him. And then one day in the middle of summer we stood outside a friend's birthday party while I threw up on the sidewalk.

It had been one of the hottest days on record in an already-boiling July. I'd left work early and canceled a promising second date with someone else, partly because I was dizzy but mostly because I couldn't think about anybody besides this boy who had taken up space in my head for so long. When Sam invited me to the party I shook off my nausea, forgot all about the heat.

In the months since he'd come back into my life I'd wanted him to see me as someone who had it together, who didn't need him or anyone to make me whole. But I hadn't eaten since lunch and the night felt no cooler than the day and so the three beers I'd drunk reappeared as we stood talking outside.

He dropped his cigarette when I bent double. He rubbed my back and stroked my hair and all I could do was let tears leak and mumble, "I don't want you to see me like this. I don't want you to see me this weak."

He looked confused. "Why not?"

I don't remember what I said. Something sputtering and unrehearsed, something about how much I cared about him and just wanted him to see me as my best self. Even then, before the fights about ambition and sex, before the frustration of him not being able to tell me what he wanted and me not being able to give it to him, before the year of sleeping curled around each other's sweat-soaked bodies and the six months of sleeping back to back, I was scared that the wind would blow the wrong way and he would leave again. I never stopped being scared. My fear would manifest itself as jealousy, as paranoia, as anger and nagging and everything but the thing it was.

And I do not know about brain chemistry but I do know that it wasn't the drinking that blurs this moment for me now, nor the years in between. It was the most raw I've ever been in front of another person, a crumpled, spitty heap asking-begging-demanding to be loved back. Something in me (maybe everything in me) shut down, so unused to this unplanned concession of control.

Whatever I said, when we woke up the next morning he was my boyfriend. We were us.

I spent so much energy over the course of our time together making and collecting totems. I embroidered Sam a sampler that said "BARF" and felt a flush of ownership every time I saw it hanging in his bedroom; I felt the same way when he'd walk around a corner wearing the knitted beanie. I inventoried our kisses and I-love-yous, reread texts and emails until I knew them half by heart. In the few photos we took, I studied our faces for evidence, I think, that we were real.

Loving someone can give you a purpose and a project. It can give you a context and therefore a clearer sense of yourself: here is who I am because here is who he is. Look at what we've made together. Look at how far we've come, the plans we've concocted, the keys we've exchanged. The hope I was capable of containing. I never shook the twisted fairy-tale idea that if Sam could just patch up a few holes, he'd be able to love me as fully and forever as I wanted him to, and that, in turn, would mend my rips as well.

Our year and a half is hazy to me now, in a different way from that first terrifying night. More like the memory of a country I visited when I was young, or a vague blanket of sensations with a few distinct moments scattered throughout: the first time we said "I love you," at my office holiday party; dancing around his living room while he blasted Fleetwood Mac on his roommate's record player; a fight at a house belonging to a family friend for whom we were taking care of an extremely old cat and a reasonably young dog. (We were always playing house with other people's pets.)

And I don't remember the beginnings of our fights, nor their causes—a few careless words, plans changed at the last minute—just where we'd end up. I'd become so convinced that his smallest gestures signified his desire to leave me, that he didn't love me the way I wanted, the way I thought I needed, the way that meant I could finally rest. Of course I never said that, out loud or to myself; of course what I wanted was impossible, and not really what I wanted at all. I was just scared, because I did not know what would happen if I had to leave this cozy, cramped place I'd helped to build. I didn't know where else to go.

But no matter how I clutched—I'm sure, partly, because of it—we grew at different rates and in different directions. The same repeated fights and disappointments wore a groove and then one night, the mushy hurt solidified into a surprisingly compact decision. This part, I remember.

It was a Sunday night. I'd returned to Brooklyn after visiting my family for Thanksgiving. We'd fought, yet again, over text, the lines so familiar it was like we'd rehearsed them. Sam came to my house. We ate spaghetti carbonara in my tiny kitchen, decided it would be right to kiss goodbye, and then he left.

In the year that followed Sam, I didn't quite know how to be. My sadness over losing him had, again, that edge of relief— there would be no more fights, no more hope hardening to dread. I could just live here, in this quiet place where I didn't have to tug, didn't have to guess at what someone who was not me really wanted. Didn't have to try and figure out what someone who *was* me really wanted.

The first month was cozy in its loneliness, the weather so

cold that there was nothing to do but hunker down in my apartment and ask Aude to sleep beside me every once in a while. Soon, though, my mind started to move in its usual patterns. I had a string of small but sharp disappointments, people who seemed promising and then abruptly (or, worse, haltingly) broke it off. I'd meet someone, we would start up, and immediately I would jump ahead to that intimate space I was so desperate to get back to. The present reality almost didn't matter: who the person was, what they said they wanted or didn't, whether I stopped to consider whether I wanted them at all.

Each new romance would start with a few weeks of cautious happiness that soon curdled into panic—why is he taking so long to reply to my text? Why did he roll over in the morning instead of reaching out for me? Sometimes I would voice these swirling thoughts but often I didn't. Instead, because I couldn't control anyone else's feelings or behavior, I'd spend that frantic energy examining myself. I looked for all the ways I was falling short: nose and teeth too big and crooked; too loud and dramatic, especially when drunk; deodorant application too infrequent; feelings too obvious; heart too easy; altogether much too much.

After all that spiraling, all that jumping, all that work just for the sake of doing work, the final break always felt like a rest. A clumsy return to the floor after weeks of frightened hovering. Whether a text or a tear-streaked conversation, whether an "I'm sorry" or "I can't" or, worst of all, "maybe one day." The finality had a horrible crunching sound but at least it had edges.

I would cry and stomp around and drink, probably too much, but at least I would *know*. At least I would belong entirely to myself again, my heart back in my chest, where it was safest, where maybe it could finally be still long enough for me to sew it back up.

Most of me is glad I never bought the yarn for Sam's sweater. (The same part that must have known even then that we might not be together come Christmas—no self-respecting knitter, no matter how speedy, would wait until after Thanksgiving to start such a gift.) I don't know what I'd do with twelve balls of gray wool now: ransack it to make a family's worth of hats and mittens? Attempt something nuts and over-the-top like an arm-chair cover or a hammock? Just let it sit there on my bookshelf, taking up more space than all the surrounding colors, reminding me of what I had, what I lost, what I will find again? That's the part of me that does wish I'd had the yarn in hand during our final weeks together, that I had started the project after all. Maybe it could have absorbed some of that hopeful-doomed magic, the last bit of proof that I was there.

Since Sam, I haven't attempted to challenge the curse. Not because I believe in it, or because there hasn't been anyone worthy—I hope to knit somebody a lovely sweater someday, the kind you see in photographs of your parents when they were young. I want to build that kind of life and to make those kinds of memories. I still want to be loved fully and forever, and to do the same right back. I just don't know the measurements for that sweater yet.

But there is one body that I know by heart. After that first year spent on my own, right after my grandmother's funeral, I bought an armload of soft gray yarn. It wasn't the type I would have used for a boyfriend sweater, not a heavy fisherman's wool, but a soft, haloed alpaca shot through with silk. I used it to knit a smaller, slimmer sweater. It's a cardigan. It has cables twining down the sides, and pockets lined with mustard yellow flannel I'd been keeping for I don't know what occasion. There was no pattern; instead, I tried it on as I went and adjusted as needed. I gave myself permission to leave mistakes if they weren't worth the trouble to fix. I sort of came to like them, those uneven little marks in the fabric, a reminder that every part of this flawed beautiful thing is mine.

As I knitted, it occurred to me that maybe the Curse of the Boyfriend Sweater *is* real, but it's not quite accurate to call it a curse. Maybe it's more of a litmus test, a method of determining whether what you have with someone is going to last. Is it solid enough to stand up under the weight of all those stitches, all that hope, all that work the two of you must choose to put in, or will it collapse before the final row?

I decorated my sweater—my Girlfriend Sweater, as I came to think of it—with pins I'd collected (one in the shape of a piece of pizza, another that looks like an envelope, a third that just reads SHUT UP), and wore it for weeks until it started to smell. I've worn it on first dates and last ones, to protests and parties, when I need a boost or just an extra layer in my freezing Manhattan office. It reminds me that sweaters that aren't the right size aren't bad, or wrong, or signs that we are bad or wrong; they just don't fit. Others will. And in the meantime, you can always make one for yourself.

Frogging, or
How to Start Over

~~~~~~~~~~~~~~~~~~~~~~~~~~~~~~~~

The hardest part of crafting isn't threading an impossibly tiny needle. It's not a complicated lace-knitting technique, nor is it working on a loom that is taller than you will ever be. It's not carpal tunnel nor a hunched back nor eyes squinting to see your work when you should have gone to bed two hours ago. Not paint fumes, not paper cuts, not even the mile-long checkout line that exists at every Michaels in North America. No: the hardest part of making anything is knowing when to start over.

Here is how it goes with knitting. You come across a pattern that grabs you, or an especially alluring ball of yarn. (Some people let the materials lead the way while others begin with the idea. I've always been pretty haphazard in my approach, which is why I own dozens of unknitted patterns and thousands of yards of unknitted yarn with no plans to ever wed the two.) You sit down in front of the TV or with a podcast in order to get through the tedious, unsatisfying beginning of any project: casting on. Getting that first row of stitches onto the needles takes the sort of counting and concentration that you are expressly trying to avoid by knitting, but until you can enlist a casting-on intern, it's a step you have to take.

The first row you knit after the cast-on is always difficult. Maybe you started too tightly and have to force your needles through the stubborn stitches, or maybe too loose and now you have to tug each strand of yarn so you don't leave any holes. The beginning is a slog.

But then, ten minutes or twenty or sometimes a week later, you look down and realize that what you have is a thing. Nothing yet identifiable as a hat or scarf, but no longer just the anemic start. You can tug it and pat it and stretch it out, and best of all, you can start to picture what it will look like when it's finally really in the world. This fixed image is enough to drive you forward long after the show you'd settled in to watch has rolled its credits.

Which is why there's a tiny apocalypse when you realize your mistake. You cast on 84 stitches when you were supposed to have only 48; you mixed up the right side and the left because who ever thinks to do that "L" hand trick after the age of, like, six? You frantically try to do some mental arithmetic that might fix it, and then when that proves too hard you rejigger your vision altogether—doesn't your sister's boyfriend have an unusually large head? They've only been dating for three weeks, but hey, everyone needs a winter hat, right? *Right????*

Then comes anger. Fuck this pattern, you think, they should have picked a bigger font, made it beyond explicit what you were *absolutely not to do.*

"Hey, [your name]!" they should have written at the top of the page. "We know you tend to zone out somewhere around the tenth row, so just a reminder that you should definitely start the ribbing by then so the whole thing doesn't look lopsided! You're great and we love you!!!"

Because just about then your anger shifts to a more immediate target: you, the hasty, clumsy moron who didn't bother to count, who somehow didn't notice when a crucial stitch was dropped two inches back. Why did you think you could do this? Why couldn't you stick to an activity you know, like biting your nails or standing in front of the open fridge for so long the lightbulb burns out? Why did you ever try to make something new?

The project, meanwhile, keeps staring at you like a puppy in a kill shelter. You can stuff it deep in your bag or hide it under your bed but you'll feel it anyway, waiting for its fate. Maybe you'll even take it out once or twice and knit a few more rows before cramming it back out of sight. Melodramatic, perhaps, but there are moments when it feels like indelible proof of your failings: you're too impatient, you tug too tightly, your execution can never live up to your ideas. In fact, the relative insignificance of a piece of knitting is proof in itself—you couldn't control something as inconsequential as this? How are you supposed to be in charge of the rest of your life?

This phase can last for minutes or months. You start other projects in the meantime; you move on to something else entirely, like softball or smoking. You forget what it was like, exactly, to stare at those particular stitches, to picture what the finished product would eventually look like.

And then one day things are different. Like after a breakup, that first morning when you wake up and realize you've forgotten to miss the person. Maybe you want the yarn for some new endeavor. Maybe you've decided that having nothing is better than having something that just isn't working.

And so you do the one thing knitters are taught never to do: you slide the stitches off the needle. It feels like a skipped heartbeat or a caught breath. Maybe there is a flash of regret—*What are you doing, you could still save this*—but it's such a quick gesture that there's no going back. For a moment the stitches look naked and silly, those little loops with nothing to give them structure. And then you take the end of the yarn and you pull. Knitters call this "frogging" because of the sound it supposedly makes: *rip-it, rip-it, rip-it*. "Rip it" sounds to me more like a command, a testament to how good it feels when you finally decide to just fucking do it.

You pull and you wind and you watch your work unknit itself in one one-thousandth of the time it took you to create it. Then you reach the end. Where once you had the thing, now you only have its materials and its memory.

The yarn will not be perfect. It will be kinked and ragged, marked with the shape it used to assume. Usually it will bounce back, though, when given enough time and maybe a little steam. It'll become something different: a pair of mittens next winter, a basket to hold more projects in the spring. A series of squares, a single strand running through a tapestry, a gift for someone you haven't met yet.

Or maybe the yarn will become exactly what you'd hoped, exactly the project you'd started in the first place. Maybe one day—right away or in a year—you'll pick up your needles and make it through the cast-on. You'll count and you'll recount, you'll hold the yarn so it doesn't choke and it doesn't flop, you'll catch the stitch you drop right away and put it back where it belongs. You'll make a few mistakes but they won't be worth ripping out.

And sooner than you expected you'll be back at the point where you abandoned the old version, and then you'll get past it, and then you'll bind off the stitches and be done. The stopping will be part of it; the restarting will be too. This time, you'll get it right.

The Best Places
to Knit, Ranked

~~~~~~~~~~~~~~~~~~~~~~~~~~~~~~~~~~~~~~

8. **The movies.** Too dark and your fingers are often greasy with popcorn residue, but still very satisfying, especially if the movie is dumb.

7. **A bar.** Also generally too dark, but it's a good conversation starter, plus you're usually up for attempting more-daring techniques after a few drinks.

6. **Waiting rooms.** Nothing good ever happens in a waiting room, but having something productive to do alleviates the boredom and, to a degree, the anxiety.

5. **In transit.** This is maybe too big a category because there are so many types of transit, with attendant pitfalls and advantages. Subranking:

   a. **The subway.** Great for catching short little moments of peace, if you can grab a seat or a spot to lean against a pole that won't cause major inconvenience to the other riders.

b. **The train (Amtrak or commuter rail).** Glorious, but so often you find yourself wanting to spend your precious in-between time doing other activities, like using the weak Wi-Fi signal to read every tweet your crush has ever posted or drinking $9 train wine or beer you smuggled in your duffel bag.

c. **Planes.** Same as above, except with the slight fear that this will be the time the TSA arbitrarily decides to confiscate your knitting needles and arrests you as some kind of fiber terrorist.

d. **Car rides.** Rad, as long as you're not the one driving.

e. **Boats.** I don't really like boats.

f. **Walking.** You actually can knit and walk, if the pattern is easy enough and you are okay with being the type of person who is knitting and walking, which I am in theory but never really think to do because there are so many other things you can do while walking, like listen to music or podcasts or contemplate your surroundings or stare at your phone wondering why your crush hasn't tweeted in three hours, is it maybe because they got a new girlfriend?

4. **Yarn stores.** Most have tables expressly for this purpose—my favorite even has a small bar at the back—and usually everyone is nice. Sometimes they'll look you up and down if you seem like a young hipster but you can't blame people for

wanting to defend their territory after the onslaught of Not Just for Grandmas™, and once they see you're one of them they warm right up.

3. **Your house.** Alone, with people, watching something, eating something. It's your house, your ways. I can't presume to know them.

2. **On vacation.**

    a. With other people.

    b. Alone. My favorite knitting experience ever took place on a solo trip. More on this in a minute.

1. **At the beach.** More on this right after that.

Moving the Needle

~~~~ ~~~~ ~~~~ ~~~~ ~~~~ ~~~~ ~~~~

Here is the story of my favorite knitting experience ever.

The summer after Sam and I broke up, I had a particularly memorable week. I had been dating a guy for a few months, the first time in my newly single life where anything had grown to the point where it could really be a *thing*. He was funny and sweet and had a British accent; on our third or fourth date, we'd had to rush his roommate's sick cat to the vet and saved her life, which was a good enough story to cement two people together, at least temporarily. I liked the idea that I could move on neatly and relatively quickly, that the world was full of possibility, that all it took was going to the right friend's karaoke party or opening up Tinder at the right moment and I could be back in the game—wanted, needed, loved.

But then he broke up with me. It was a Tuesday. On Wednesday, sad and anxious and wanting a task, I went to urgent care;

I'd woken up earlier in the week with a large round bruise on my thigh that I had no memory of getting, and rather than healing, it was getting worse, its edges purpling and the veins in the center becoming more and more prominent. The bruise had been described variously by friends who had seen it as "gnarly," "vicious," and "Whoa, doesn't it kind of look like the night sky from this angle?" I figured it was time to get a professional opinion.

As an inveterate hypochondriac, I was almost relieved when the doctor seemed alarmed by the bruise—I wasn't just fretting for the sake of it! I was less relieved when he said that it could be a blood clot. I had, in the course of my nighttime Internet trawling, discovered that blood clots could turn into something called "deep vein thrombosis," which could travel elsewhere in your body and kill you. I did not want to die, and so I spent the next two days running around Manhattan leaving vials of my blood at various facilities. It was, at least, a nice distraction from the breakup (which one, I couldn't tell you), and from the general stagnation of my life. It wasn't that this boy had made me truly happy, but he had been something to think about, to build toward, proof that I wasn't going to wander in tight circles forever. Now there was nothing.

On Thursday afternoon, while I was at work, I got a call from an unknown number.

Ugh, I thought, bracing myself for news of my own impending dramatic death. *This is it.*

But it wasn't one of the testing centers. Nor was it the British boy, calling to declare his undying love for me, nor Sam, breaking the silence that had sprung up ever since we'd parted ways. No, instead it was my agent, with the news that I had sold this book.

I usually find it self-indulgent and time-consuming when writers get all meta, so feel free to skip ahead until the following page if that is also true for you. But all I had ever really wished for was this. Yes, I'd wished for boyfriends and jobs and apartments, and for the people I love to be happy and healthy, and for democracy not to crumble in my lifetime. Above all, though, I wanted to make something that was mine, something that could stretch further than a sweater and mean more than a stack of embroideries. I'd been writing my whole life, from my knockoff *Harriet the Spy*–style notebook scribblings of everything my friends and family were doing to the essays and articles I wrote for the website I worked for. Writing was—is—how I make sense of the world, and like crafting, I can do it without permission, without waiting, entirely on my own.

But it was still exciting and terrifying to realize that other people would soon read what I had to say too, that I would have the chance to collect the bits and pieces of my life and weave them together, see what they looked like as a messy but cohesive whole. And so I hung up the phone, and I poked at my bruise, which—spoiler alert—did not wind up traveling to my brain or lungs to kill me, because it was just a regular bruise, albeit a big one of mysterious origin, and then I asked my boss if I could take off the following week and go to Montreal.

I don't quite know what possessed me to go on a trip, the first I would ever take alone. I'm not a spontaneous person, if that hasn't been made exceedingly clear yet; I don't like to spend a lot of money or rearrange my schedule. I was already living on my own, so it wasn't that I needed to evade roommates, and despite the ever-present eau de hot trash, I actually like New York in the summertime, with its rooftops and empty weekends. Maybe I wanted to run away from myself and all my attendant worries, at least for a couple of days; maybe I wanted to run away from everything else, to help myself get back to me.

I do, however, know why I chose Montreal. Proximity, for one thing—I could take a train all the way from Penn Station, without needing to board a plane. Expense, for another—the train ticket cost around $120 round-trip, and the small but lovely apartment I found on Airbnb cost less even than that per night. And finally, familiarity—I'd been once before, with my college boyfriend.

Hirschey and I had taken the train up during a break from school. On the first night I became convinced I had meningitis, because my neck was extremely stiff and I felt feverish and some college student somewhere had, I think, just died suddenly of it so it stood to reason that I would too. Anxiety is nothing if not narcissistic.

Hirschey, so kind and worried, hailed a Canadian cab and we went to the Canadian emergency room. We were in and out in twenty minutes, because Canadian health care is amazing and also because I did not have meningitis (that might have slowed things down somewhat).

I wanted to go back to Montreal on my own because, I told myself, we hadn't really done it right. From what I recalled we mostly went to bars near our hostel and drank Labatt Blue without being carded. I wanted to do it differently, on my own, without having someone to slow me down or save me. I wanted to go somewhere that felt far away even though almost everyone spoke English. And certain places feel like they belong permanently to certain times and certain people, and sometimes you just decide it's time to make them yours again. I hadn't been able to do that yet with Sam's neighborhood, below the park, nor with the various bars and restaurants around the city I'd visited with all those not-quite-there boys. I would, instead, cross borders.

So I booked the Amtrak ticket and the Airbnb. Twelve hours is a long ride, but all of a sudden I had a purpose. I had a book to start writing; I had a strange blue cotton jumper thingy I'd been seized with the urge to knit, even though the longer I spent with it the more it looked like it would have been better suited for a toddler. I liked that I was making something a little ridiculous, something that nobody in the world would think to ask for; it made me feel slightly better about striking out and starting to write something that, in my deepest heart, I worried would be the same.

I don't think I wrote at all on my way up. I watched a lot of *Sex and the City* on my laptop, and thought about the boy and the book and the bruise, and looked out the window at an increasing number of cows and lakes. (This may not seem like an efficient way to fill twelve hours, but it's amazing how much space self-pity mixed with self-satisfaction can consume.)

When I arrived in Montreal, though, all other thoughts evaporated as soon as I got to an ATM. I hadn't thought to bring cash—I'd just take some out when I arrived, I'd reasoned, and skip all the cumbersome cash exchange rates—and yet now my debit card wasn't working. I tried my credit card; same thing. The machine kept telling me it was unreadable; when I attempted to buy a bottle of water at a nearby kiosk, the woman behind the counter told me the same thing. After trying one more newsstand and two more ATMs, I called my bank. It took twenty minutes to get through to a human, who kindly informed that, oh yes, this happened sometimes in Canada because of "inconsistencies with chip technology." I did not really know what that meant, and still don't, and asked her what to do so that I could have access to my money in the next five days.

"You could always find someone to take out cash for you!" I believe she said. I can't exactly remember, because right around then came my panic blackout.

You have to understand that this was my first trip alone. Of course I'd traveled by myself before, but always to meet up with my family or coworkers; there was an endpoint to the aloneness, people waiting at the other end to help me. The one time I'd ever missed a connecting flight, I cried until the airline booked me a free room at the Miami Holiday Inn Express. I was nineteen years old, but the flirty waiter at the hotel restaurant let me order a glass of red wine without checking my ID.

But until Montreal, I had never really planned a trip. I hadn't studied abroad in college, hadn't traveled after graduation like so many of the people I grew up with. In fact, I'd sort of looked sideways at the whole business—it smelled strongly of escapism to me, of ducking the life you were supposed to be building in favor of a brief, expensive fantasy. I preferred to think of myself as someone who built homes where she was, who could take any dorm room, any life path, and make it her own. I couldn't see the point in investing, especially temporarily, in anywhere else.

I'm glad I decided to stay where I was back then. I made some fantastic friends in that quiet semester when so many people were gone. I entered and won the writing contest where I met Marina, which indirectly led to that internship in New York, which indirectly led to where I am now. My fear can be useful. It focuses me and makes me decisive, flags me when something truly is wrong. But it's also limiting, knee-jerk, and makes me averse to any situation where I don't know the outcome, because it means having to give up that most precious thing: control.

Which, it turns out, yeah! That's kind of the point of traveling! Here is what happened when I finally left the Montreal train station, tear-streaked and laden with my luggage. (I'd planned to take a cab to the place where I was staying, but you can't take a cab without money.) I walked the mile or so there. I texted the girl from whom I was renting the apartment. I told her that I knew it seemed weird, and I wouldn't be at all offended if she said no, but if she could take out some cash for me (I'd pay her via PayPal or via the checkbook that I was blessedly carrying, since I'd boarded the train straight from a therapy appointment) I would be eternally grateful.

She did. Her name was Ariane, and we liked each other so much from our brief transaction that we decided to meet for drinks later in the week. I'd reached out to a former classmate, whom I hadn't thought to contact when I was planning the trip, and he did the same—spotted me the money and invited me to a party. All of a sudden this quiet, solo trip I'd planned was peppered with engagements, which turned into more when I met some girls my age. I spent a lot of time with them, and a lot of time by myself, and I ate so many bagels. Did you know that bagels are best as a drunk nighttime food? I didn't, until Montreal. Montreal bagels are thin and cost nothing, especially if you factor in the exchange rate. I bought a tub of cream cheese and it was the only thing I kept in my borrowed fridge, and every night after eating and drinking and talking to wonderful strangers I would buy a bagel from the famous twenty-four-hour spot around the corner. I would eat it at the dining-room table, dunking it directly into the cream cheese because there was nobody watching to tell me that was gross. I knitted my jumper and did not look at my phone and fell asleep each night so, so happy.

That solo trip gave way to more. Not a lot, but enough. I went to Berlin for a week and ate a lot of bread and cheese and mastered the subway; I spent a month writing and housesitting at a beachside mansion in Rhode Island, during a deserted February when I spoke to almost no one. I flew out to San Francisco to see a great friend for a memorial service and wound up kissing the good, kind boy who I am still with now. I learned that I like my own company, my own rhythms, even outside the circumscribed life I'd built for myself in New York. I like waking up early and locating a place that will serve me a sandwich or salad before ten a.m.; I like doing yoga when I want, writing when I want, walking down a snowy beach with a fur coat and a glass of Chardonnay, *Grey Gardens*–style, when I want. Above all, I like knowing that I can save myself, or can at least drum up the courage to call upon others when I need it. The world doesn't need to end even when I'm outside mine.

It's not like a few days in Montreal precipitated all of this; maybe I would have seen Germany anyway, would still have told the boy I thought he was cute. But it did move the needle. I spent my last afternoon in a yarn store I'd read about, a place I'd planned to pop into for only a few minutes. Instead, the owner and I got to talking, and then she offered me a cup of tea, which turned into an entire pot and an afternoon spent knitting the jumper, the light going gold and then fading outside. I can't even remember the name of the store—it was in French, which I still do not speak despite the efforts of Aude and the Needham High School French exchange program—but I remember how calm I felt, like I was exactly where I was supposed to be and it was all because I'd made a series of decisions to get myself there. I deliberated for almost an hour over a skein of silk-and-linen yarn (it cost more than any meal I'd bought over the course of the week) and then finally relented: its color matched the brilliant light, exactly what I pictured as a child when I read "Rumpelstiltskin," as he spins straw into gold. I think he gets a bad rap in that story: at least he took nothing and helped someone turn it into something.

I brought the yarn on the twelve-hour trip back to New York, where right away I set to work making it into a large, lacy shawl. *That* was my favorite knitting experience, even more so than sitting in the Montreal yarn store: it cemented the idea that I could keep that feeling of belonging and rightness and take it with me even when I left a place. I wasn't who I was because I'd amassed enough tokens—a job, an apartment, a boy—or none at all. I could step outside of all those things and still keep that essential core. I could still make friends and write words and build nests, however temporary. I could still knit a beautiful lacy shawl.

Lace is a funny thing up close, just a series of elegant, ordered holes. Lace patterns, at first, appear as unintelligible shorthand (ssk? sk2p? wtf?), and if you choose to go all in and attempt to read a chart, it resembles nothing so much as a blueprint for a very ugly apartment building. Once you get it in your head, though, it's extremely satisfying, a game of trading—if you add a stitch here, you need to subtract one somewhere else. I made my shawl on the fumes of that trip and when it was done I draped it over the back of my couch, where it still lives. I never finished the blue jumper. I decided I didn't really need it after all.

Okay, So Here Is Why Summer Is the Best Time for Knitting

1. You tend to travel more in the summer, so there's more time to kill in transit. I'm often asked if I'm worried about the TSA taking away my needles, which has never been a problem, although it's sort of nuts that they don't let you bring, like, lip gloss unless it's cordoned off in a plastic bag, but you are allowed a bundle of sharp metal sticks? America.

2. And if someone (read: a dude) is taking up more than their fair share of the plane armrest, a subtle way to take revenge is by needleworking wildly enough that your elbow jiggles theirs. This is a summertime corollary to the year-round manspreader-repellent properties of crafting, usually deployed on subways or buses.

3. Suddenly everyone seems to be wearing these effortless, lacy tops and dresses and cover-ups. You can make those!

Crochet was basically invented for this purpose, but there are plenty of simple, summery knitting patterns too. It's not just for bundling up with beside a roaring fire or whatever.

4. It's the perfect beach activity. You have to plan your project carefully, of course: nothing wool, no intricate patterns. Stick to cotton or linen. I've had great luck with headbands or simple shawls (the question of whether you *need* a knitted headband or shawl is another thing entirely)—something to keep you interested but not so engrossed that you can't carry on a conversation.

5. If you're feeling especially ambitious and a pattern is mindless enough, you can read at the same time. (This does require clean, dexterous feet.) Otherwise, it's enough just to look at the water and match the rhythm of your stitches to the waves.

6. In my favorite photo of myself I'm sitting on the beach knitting a small yellow cardigan. I remember being very anxious that day—it was right before I was set to move into my own apartment for the first time, when I could barely brush my teeth in the morning because that small action could trigger nauseated panic attacks. Still, in that photo I am smiling so big, happy to be resting for a minute, happy to be there. Miraculously I was still in New York City, just a very long subway ride from home. There's something more open about the warmer months even when things are hard, this sense that you can move more freely and nothing weighs as much. It's never been the time when I can undertake huge, sustained

projects, but I tend to listen better to my small impulses, those bursts of creative energy it's easy to ignore the rest of the year. Maybe it's residue from camp, or leftover relief-nostalgia about no longer being in school; maybe it hits everyone at a different time. For me, it's always been in summer.

7. There's a small thrill in incongruity—who *knits* at the *beach*? *You* could!

Learning Curves

~~~~~~

"Jesus fucking Christ."

"Aude, shhh."

"I keep stabbing myself with the fucking thing."

"Here, no, wait, let me do that."

"Seriously, fuck this fucking shit."

I don't usually care when Aude swears, but we're in a tiny, elegant boutique, surrounded by people I barely know and whom she's just met. They're crafters, mostly, people I know from the Internet and through my job writing about DIY stuff; I was invited to this embroidery workshop by one of them, and perhaps somewhat ill-advisedly brought Aude along. Even though I know crafters to be a vibrant, accepting bunch, I'd prefer my best friend not yell "*Fuck!*" around them too much.

We're both hunched over a single pair of black pants as she

struggles to poke an embroidery needle through the waistband. I've shown her the basics and immediately she jumps right into a big project: stitching the word "Player" in gold thread. It's hard work, maneuvering the needle through that thick double layer of fabric. But Aude has never been one to avoid something just because it's hard.

We met at a publishing course the summer after we graduated college, which was neither a time when nor a place where I expected to meet a best friend. And I especially didn't expect to meet *this* best friend.

There were 102 of us, mostly women, nearly all immediately out of school. We were stuffed in an overly air-conditioned lecture hall for nine hours a day, and I knitted through almost all of them. We were anxious and eager and everything was so heightened it was amazing you couldn't smell it. Because what we wanted were jobs. We were happy to learn, and to have a reason to be in the city with something to do once we'd been cut adrift from our various academic institutions, but the endgame, gleaming quietly in some eyes and on fire in others, was to Get. Fucking. Hired.

I was happy to be there. Or maybe it's more that I was relieved. College had been my place—the only school I'd applied to, exactly the right size at around 2,400 students, exactly the right distance at three and a half hours away from home. I'd shown up my first week and instantly fallen in friend-love with the people on my hall, the members of my all-female a cappella group, my (mostly) laid-back but (generally) brilliant classmates. I loved the trees that lined the long drive up to the Main Building and the old-fashioned Gothic architecture of the library. I loved writing papers and throwing parties with themes like "Geometry" and "America" and developing sudden, painful crushes that sometimes culminated in sweaty two a.m. tussles in twin-size beds. But mostly what I loved was the sense of who I was. I liked being known—as the girl with dyed-red hair and choir-girl posture, as the humor editor and the beatboxer, as a frequent hand raiser and earnest advice giver and loud drunk. Even when the self-contained bubble of the campus got to be claustrophobic, even when I got sick of going to the same parties and kissing the same people and reading the same essays, it was always exactly the right size for me.[1]

And so when I had to leave it at the end of four years, I didn't quite know who I was or where to go; all of a sudden I'd reached the end of a road I'd comfortably plodded along for my entire life. My friends were off to grad school and DC and Indonesia, some to start their forever-lives, some just testing out new detours until they figured out what they wanted, no longer just a few doors or a dining-hall dinner away.

I'd liked New York when I'd interned there the summer before, but without a job or a reason to be in the city, it didn't

---

[1] I was assigned Walter Benjamin's *Art in the Age of Mechanical Reproduction* for three separate classes.

make sense to just pack up and go back there. So I applied to this course because, hey, I liked books and words, and I applied to a lot of random entry-level jobs that I did not hear back from. Two weeks after my mother moved me out of my college apartment she turned around and drove me to New York, a hundred miles to the south, never once complaining.

The first thing I did when I got to this new, far more porous campus was set up my room. I'd been fastidious about my spaces in college—my mother and I installed curtains, swapped out the horrible dorm light fixtures, and drove the same green rug back and forth for years until a roommate threw up on it and it was finally retired—and so even though I'd only be in this shared grad-student housing for six weeks, I needed to feel like something was mine. I taped postcards above the desk and bought a basil plant from the hardware store across the street. It didn't survive the summer.

I met other students at lectures and in the dining hall and we sized one another up. They were like remixed versions of the people I'd come to love, only without the benefit of time to soften their quirks and habits into fuzzier, more forgiving versions of themselves. Instead, each foible became a stand-in, to my anxious mind, for entire personalities: the iPad-wielding note takers in the front row were type-A try-too-hards, the handful of boys scattered at the back were conniving jerks out to seduce the horde of frenzied women. And, look, we were none of us our best selves that summer—too heightened, too uncertain, too torn between figuring out what we wanted and presenting that we knew exactly what to do. Too eager to come to conclusions about people we knew almost nothing about, because it seemed easier than admitting we didn't know ourselves very well either. And everyone, me extremely included, *was* kind of insufferable.

I made friends with a girl who liked to sit in the second row, like me (not as try-too-hard as the blazer wearers in the front row, but still close enough that our glowing, competent faces would be noticed), and then with a girl who had dyed-red hair just like mine. Lines formed to mob visiting lecturers before they'd even pushed back their chairs onstage; the second a new job listing was emailed out to the group there was an audible whoosh of unemployed honor-roll students rushing back to their laptops. We listened to book editors and magazine publicists talk about how they spent their days, and imagined how we would one day spend ours, and every time someone mentioned the runaway success of *Fifty Shades of Grey* (that summer's blockbuster and the purported future savior of the publishing industry), we made tally marks in our notebooks, and took that number of gulps at the bar later.

And then came the résumé workshop. "Miriam is scary," we'd heard in whispers from people who knew people. "Miriam takes no shit whatsoever." Miriam was the career counselor who would be critiquing our résumés and cover letters, some of which clocked in north of three pages.

I liked her immediately. She was no-bullshit, had no time for pontificating about what a company could do for you and no interest in your summer lifeguarding job. In her care our material became, harshly and without ceremony, leaner.

"I have a question," Miriam said during one of her talks to the group. She held up a piece of paper, clearly some poor student's résumé. We all silently prayed it wasn't ours, but all résumés look the same from fifteen feet back. "Which of you listed under your Interests section, um"—she consulted it—"'fire-breathing'?"

There was silence. Then a girl sitting all the way at the back of the room raised her hand. "I'm also a pretty good stilt-walker," she said. Her voice was husky and could have been ironic, but she didn't seem to be making fun of anyone, not even herself.

"Huh," Miriam said, because that's all there was to say. "What's your name?"

"Aude-like-'Ode-to-Joy,'" the girl said in a single breath. "It's French." When she stood up to answer, her short brown hair and small pointed nose were visible. She did not seem afraid. Miriam seemed pleased by this answer and offered a couple of tweaks to the résumé, but the fire-breathing, it seemed, would stay.

After that day I noticed her everywhere. *Who is this bitch?* I wondered, like I had with Marina the year before. *Who comes to a place like this, so polished and airless, and still manages to be so truly* herself? So what if she spoke fluent French, and had been raised in Brooklyn, and had enormous boobs and a wardrobe of crisp white button-downs and a ubiquitous pack of cigarettes? Nobody could be that self-possessed. I thought that she had to be faking it.

I'm bad at first impressions. Not making them—I know how to smile and ask questions in all the right places; I've always been good at charming adults and teachers and first dates—but reading them is another story. I'm often repelled by the same people I'll later come to love, or, worse, drawn to ones I soon won't be able to stand. I'm so quick to slot new people into defined spaces that I'm wrong about them a lot of the time; I want them to be boyfriends or best friends or nemeses as soon as we're through with introductions, and for them to see me the same way.

But, thank God, one day Aude-like-"Ode-to-Joy" joined me and Anne (fellow second-row enthusiast) and Liz (faux redhead) for lunch, and I realized just how much I wanted her in my zone.

The four of us spent the rest of that summer in a hermetic, cackling huddle, eating our lunch on the tiny porch outside the dining hall while two of us pined over boys who didn't deserve it, one of us cooed in sympathy, and one of us (guess who) offered dismissive remarks between drags on her cigarette. I applied for exactly one publishing job and wanted it so badly, if only so I could feel needed again. I found out that I didn't get it at the bar after class; someone else from the course had. I ran back to my room in tears and Aude bought me a beer the next day.

"Fuck them," she said. "Fuck that. You're going to be so much happier."

And then the six weeks were up, and we'd given our résumés to everyone we encountered and were still no closer to a paycheck, and Aude invited me to come stay at her parents' house in Brooklyn. They would be in France for the month, she told me, visiting family, and she could use help feeding the cats and watering the plants. It's probably the kindest lie I've ever been told.

So I packed up my postcards and threw out my basil plant and moved in. To a beautiful townhouse in a Brooklyn neighborhood I hadn't heard of before that summer, alongside Prospect Park and resembling not New York so much as the New England suburb where I'd grown up. I slept in Aude's middle sister's room—when I found out she was the oldest of three girls, I was whatever the opposite of shocked is—and we spent our days avoiding the heat wave and applying for whatever jobs we could find. (Well, I did, in manic spurts; Aude was more measured in her approach, and spent a lot of time scowling and drawing in her notebook on the couch.) We ate a staggering amount of American cheese.

We fought a lot. She got cranky and withdrawn in the face of figuring out what to do with our lives while I got shrill and accusatory, and more than once we found ourselves yelling on the street, neither of us able to remember the catalyst. But we started to notice a strange thing happening. We always got through these fights and came out better than we were before. We reached tiny epiphanies: "Oh, when you say that, you actually mean this." "Ah, I get it, that wasn't a question that called for an answer."

The more often it occurred, the better we got at closing the gap between the initial flare-up and the eventual understanding. We learned to jump to that part almost right away. We learned to speak each other's language and started to put together one of our own. We learned each other's methods of performing in front of other people, especially when we were uncomfortable or uncertain: the Aude Show was blasé but provocative, studded with references to its proprietor's (frankly amazing) boobs, while the Alanna Show was high-pitched and smiley to the point of creepiness.

"EVERYTHING IS SO GREAT!!!!" I'd chirp.

"Yeah, whatever," Aude would mutter.

The truth of us is somewhere in between. She is hopeful and sensitive, able to pick up on my moods sometimes even before I can. And I was not raised in Brooklyn nor am I fluent in French, but I can find my strength and my resolve too.

After a month of cohabitation I got a job. It wasn't one of the jobs we'd been pointed toward by the course, no phones to answer or manuscripts to read. Instead it was at a website, one I'd seen popping up more and more on my Facebook feed but hadn't really thought about until they posted a listing for their new women's lifestyle section. The Wild West of the Internet looked like the sort of place where you could basically do whatever you wanted until someone told you to stop, you burned out, or your company abruptly shuttered, whichever came first. Aude was the one who told me it was okay to want something a little different, a little to the left of what we'd been preparing for. She would wind up taking a similar kind of job, in communications for a magazine.

With a small but steady source of income, I moved to an apartment just a ten-minute walk from Aude's house. She gamely mounted the five flights of stairs to my new place, even helped me carry an air conditioner all the way up. (She liked to take off her shirt whenever we'd reach the top floor, I think to the chagrin of my roommates.) She was as much my person as ever, maybe more once we had to make the continual choice to see each other.

And we did—over the next handful of years we cemented our status as a couple of sorts. Even when we aren't in relationships, it feels like a lie to say that either of us is single—we always have the other to sleep in our beds, to do the crossword with, to share beers and burgers and advice we'd be better off giving to ourselves. We are anxious a lot of the time, and we get hurt a lot too—we both fall for people easily, expect a lot, pore over text messages and parse silences for evidence of our desirability, for proof that one day soon we will not be so lonely. We worry about our families and our jobs. Usually, thankfully, these moods do not overlap; one of us will fret while the other comforts, reminds her that we've both been here before and that it will pass, that we are just as loved and good as ever, that boys are supremely bad at feelings and that we will probably not be fired because of a poorly worded email. In the rare moments when our anxieties do spring up at the same time, we're still capable of looking at the other and regarding her the way she really is—tough, kind, able to spiral ever closer to what she wants—even if we can't do that for ourselves.

"Where's Aude?" people ask when I show up to parties without her. We tweet at each other all day long even though we should be doing our jobs, even though we could just as easily text, even though we know it's irritating as hell. We still like to put on a bit of a show. We still feel so relieved to have found ourselves living solidly in our lives, and to have found someone who can see the other so clearly, that we have to say the words aloud and often to make it feel real.

One day, a few years into our grown-up lives, Aude asked me to re-teach her how to knit; she'd learned when she was younger, she said, but had fallen out of practice.

I've taught a lot of people how to make a lot of things: eight- and nine-year-olds at the performing arts day camp where I spent a decade of summers, coworkers during work hours and outside of them, friends sprawled on blankets at the park near my apartment. It's how I cement old friendships and establish new ones. It's a more diffuse identity than I had in school but I've come to like being known in this way—as the person in the office who can fix your button if it pops off, as the one you email if you want an embroidered song lyric as a last-minute wedding gift, as the triage nurse who can fix a dropped stitch or reassure you that no, you're totally right, just keep doing what you're doing. It means that I have a place and a purpose, and that I am, in some small way, needed.

Aude brought over deceptively beautiful brown alpaca yarn and a set of circular needles. I showed her how to cast on, and how to do the knit stitch, and how to reverse it in order to purl. There was some swearing, but not like during the embroidery, because in knitting there are fewer opportunities to draw blood. We drank a lot of wine. By the time she left, she had the beginnings of a cowl.

She gave that first cowl away, and the next one too. I went on to teach her youngest sister, who took to knitting in a way Aude never did. That's fine—Aude has her drawing, which she does in small moments at bars or on lazy weekend afternoons. Whenever I see her pages and pages of work I feel this shock tinged with recognition, the same way you're surprised when you walk past a surface you didn't realize was mirrored and catch your own reflection. She draws small, everyday things: a woman waiting for the subway, a tipped-over trash can on a street corner. Each picture has its own quiet, intense energy; you can't look at them just once.

One year she drew her legs every single day, sometimes in painstaking detail, sometimes in a few quick strokes. Every now and then a part of my leg or skirt made it into a drawing. I liked spotting them in her notebook. Oh, that's right, I'd think. That's where I am.

I finish embroidering the "Player" pants for her in that small boutique, mostly to keep her from shouting any more profanities but also because I love doing it, and I love her, and she wants them to exist. Sometimes it's as simple as that.

After leaving, chances are we spend the day in our usual manner: wandering around the city, popping in and out of thrift stores, splitting beers and burgers, seeing our other friends and staying at parties for no longer than fifteen minutes each. Maybe we swing by one of our houses, for naps and showers and a moment of shared quiet before reentering the world. Maybe we go our separate ways and plan to meet up again later. My days with Aude run together, because there have been so many and because there will, with any luck, be so many more.

Sixish

~~~~~~

I have plenty of ways to tell time. In the roughly four hundred square feet that my home comprises, I have an oven, a microwave, a computer, an iPad, and a phone, all of which prominently and insistently display digits whenever I look at them. (To varying degrees of accuracy—has a microwave clock ever, in the history of time, *really* been right?) I own two physical calendars at home and one at work, not to mention the Google calendar that syncs to all my iDevices and carves up my days into neat, hour-long chunks. But there are times when I crave something less neat, less harsh, less broadcast to me by an unfeeling satellite millions of miles away. I want a method of measuring that is warmer and that is mine. I want not six, but sixish.

This is, of course, a little ridiculous. Six is how you board a train before it departs and how you and your friend arrive at a restaurant when you both agree to. Six is how school works, and jobs, and any part of society that requires more than one person to do a task at a given moment. Six is for grown-ups, while sixish patently is not.

But being a grown-up can be such a drag. I'm not scared of time, exactly, but I do resent it. It frustrates me, it restrains me, and then it lurches past without a chance to catch up. It forces me to contend with it in unappetizing dollops: how long until I graduate, how long until I find a home or a job or a person, how long until I finally one day arrive at where and who I've always wanted—always waited—to be? I'm impatient. I'm ready to be done. I'm ready to *have* done, and time is always the sluggish, impassive obstacle between here and there.

And then time can be so slippery and so violent. It can present itself as a doorway that you trip through and suddenly everything is different: someone you love is gone forever, something has been said or done that can't be swallowed back down. You turn around and scrabble frantically at the doorway but it's sealed itself shut, and time—so nimble and effortless just the instant before—is back to its stony measuredness, marching you farther and farther away from the place you are screaming to get back to. Time can take the small amount of stability, the tiny measure of happiness, the hint of control you've managed to stockpile and twist them right before your eyes. Time does not have to care.

So I decided to make a clock. Maybe forty-eight hours elapsed between when I had the idea and when I hung the finished product above my front door. And if time is something that scares you or stresses you out, you should try making one too.

It's not as hard as it sounds—clockworks are easy to find. You can get a set on Amazon or at Michaels or at Jo-Ann Fabric, hands included, for around $8. It's a steal, if you think about it: this little hunk of gears and metal capable of taking the measure of every day you spend worrying, every hour you spend ignoring the things you are supposed to be doing, every minute that means the difference between perfect spaghetti carbonara and sad scrambled eggs dripping off some noodles, all yours for the price of a glass of wine.

Once you have the mechanism, you need to make your clock face. It could be a hunk of wood or a paper plate. It could be one of those modern clocks that has no face at all, just the hands in the middle and numbers stuck to the wall around it. The face should be strong enough to support the weight of the clockwork, and not so thick you can't poke through the little doohickey[1] that holds the hands. It has to be something you'll want to look at every morning and every night, and that won't seem tedious or twee if you move houses or if someone else joins you in yours. It has to be a clock that you will still like even when time has passed. It does not have to be round.

My clock, however, is round. I made it out of an embroidery

---

[1] Actual technical term.

hoop, with off-white fabric stretched tight between the two rings of wood. (If you think you've never seen one before, just picture a Jane Austen heroine sitting in a drawing room, impatiently awaiting a suitor and trying to keep her hands busy. Yeah, it's that thing.) Whereas I'm technically pretty good at knitting, I make up embroidery as I go; my stitches are uneven and the backs of my hoops look like a convention of multicolored spiders was massacred without warning. I never really formally learned, mostly just played around with thread the same way I did with yarn, although I once attended a craft camp for grown-ups in Brooklyn and had my form corrected by an extremely wonderful teacher I'm still in touch with to this day.

And so I stitched the numbers around the edges of the clock, spelled out in lowercase—"one," "nine," "eleven"—in my own friendly, crooked handwriting. I attached the clockwork through the center (had to MacGyver a backing out of the cardboard Amazon box it was delivered in) and hung it above the door of my apartment. I like the softness of the thread alongside the straight edges of the clock's hands. I even like that the numbers aren't evenly spaced, because I eyeballed their placement. Six is definitely not directly across from twelve, but it's close enough. Sixish.

I've made maybe a hundred embroideries in the past seven or so years. I started off stitching expressions I liked—none of that

"Home Is Where the Heart Is" stuff but odd little lines or sayings that stuck in my craw. The first was something I heard in an introductory art history lecture, a sentence attributed to Cézanne: "With an apple I will astonish Paris." I didn't totally know what it meant (I was busy crocheting my college boyfriend a sweater and playing a word game called *TextTwist* on my laptop), but I liked the way the words fit together, confident and surprising and exploding one after the other.

Not long after, I read this Carl Sagan quote, a favorite of nerds and coffee mugs: "If you wish to make an apple pie from scratch, you must first invent the universe." It only made sense to embroider each of them onto its own hoop, along with a third, simple picture of an apple. I absolutely misconstrued both quotes—I took my tableau to mean "I can do anything, including take over Paris and the universe while making A+ apple pies," which is the epitome of liberal-arts freshman-hood—but that's almost part of the point; with embroidery, you're capturing something free-floating and sitting with it, placing it in a new, soft context. I'm not saying you should go around misinterpreting famous thinkers, but there is something to be said for making something yours. Either way, I've taken the three hoops with me everywhere I've lived since then.

Now I make embroideries for my apartment the way some people get tattoos. (Although one is more permanent, both involve needles and sometimes bloodshed.) I've made reminders for roommates:

Don't forget:
  Keys
  Phone
  Wallet
  Recycling

And just for myself:

Do less:
  Drinking
  Worrying
  Self-flagellating

Do more:
  Knitting
  Writing
  Yoga
  Being here now

When Marina died I stitched my favorite quote of hers, the last few lines from a poem she wrote at school: "Everything is so beautiful and so short." There was no quote for Jamie, so when he died a year later I just moved hers right next to my bed. It didn't make them feel any closer, but it helped to know that I wouldn't forget.

And then not so long ago I tried an experiment. I was in an especially anxious period and noticed that my usual brain-yelling was coming through more clearly than usual, coalescing into repetitive anti-mantras: *"Don't feel that." "You are not enough." "Why you?"* They took up so much room in my head and, what's more, they were *boring*, swirling around again and again and again. I thought that maybe if I could pin them down, like an old-timey butterfly collector, these words would lose some of their power.

So I treated them the way I did any other song lyric or famous quotation. I wrote them out in pencil, on fabric stretched across a variety of hoops, and one by one I embroidered them. There were seven in all. Each took about an hour to complete, which was exactly enough time to get so thoroughly sick of whatever was written in front of me that it had to shrink, had to be stripped of its context. They seemed ridiculous, these things I said to myself; some of them even directly contradicted each other. How could "YOU ARE NOT ENOUGH" reasonably hang on a wall beside "YOU ARE MUCH TOO MUCH" and make any kind of sense?

I enjoyed dressing them up in swirly fonts and studding them with tiny stars and flowers. I liked taking this amorphous, menacing collection of voices that thrived in the darkest part of my brain and forcing them into the open. There, they shriveled.

It didn't solve anything, of course—if I'd discovered that an hour of embroidery could fix the insidious ways we dismantle ourselves, this would be a very different type of book, and I would have a lot more money and a much nicer apartment—but it brought some of my fears down to eye level. Projects, even the kind that are not so emotionally loaded, always feel smaller when they're done, when you're not obsessing over individual components anymore. The same is true for spans of time: happy periods, mourning periods—all of them flatten when you can look back on them from arm's length, when you can hold them in your hands and stick them to the wall, when you can look at them in the context of your life.

Before the clock, I'd never used embroidery to make something with an actual function. All of my pieces, even the ones on which I fought miniature battles, were meant to be decorative, hung over doorways or propped up on desks. The clock wasn't like the anti-embroideries, where the very process of capturing those words was enough to sand down their edges, at least a little. A second is still a second; a minute is still a minute; a week still feels way too long and a year still feels much too short. Some fabric and thread were never going to change that.

If anything, it's a reminder. (A very literal one: even if it's imprecise it still lets me know when I am most definitely going to be late to work.) It ticks away in my quiet apartment but its pulses aren't unkind. It's a little goofy, a little lopsided, like if Don Quixote had painted flowers on the blades of the windmills instead of charging toward them.[2] Just because you can't defeat something doesn't mean you can't make a wry sort of peace with it. And it reminds me that even if I can't ask the world to be less rigid, less unforgiving, I can ask that of myself. I can stop getting so angry when someone is twenty minutes late or takes two hours to text me back, can cease thinking of them as uncaring or careless when really the only true culprit is life, and also the New York City subway system. I can stop myself from panicking when I do the same in turn. I can learn to sit with the moments I have instead of hoarding them, worrying there won't be enough for later. I can, if I choose, if everyone else agrees—and so far, they always do—make plans for sixish.

---

[2] I'm borrowing again; my understanding of *Don Quixote* stretches only as far as LiveJournal, the online blogging community I belonged to when I was an early teen. There was a drop-down menu of emotions where you could choose how you were feeling on a given day, and "quixotic" was one of the options. I looked it up and liked it very much, the same way I like my apple trilogy.

Things I Do Wrong,
at Least as Far as
Crafting Is Concerned

1. Hold the yarn.

There are all kinds of methods for how to wrap yarn around your fingers while you knit or crochet, so that it's right there every time you need to make a stitch (that is, fairly frequently). There's the English style and the Continental/European style, which both sound like they involve a salad fork and a hostile takeover. I do not do either of them. Instead, I sort of just let the yarn . . . hang. When I need it (again, roughly twenty times a minute) I pick it back up and toss it over my needle. This is, obviously, extremely inefficient, but each time I've tried to teach myself the "right" way I find it so slow that I get frustrated and revert to my incorrect yet familiar method. I can do it quickly and without looking, so I think this is about it for me. I wish I could remember exactly how my grandmother held her yarn—

not so I can blame her for teaching me that way, but so I can know if this slapdash approach of mine at least has some history. Maybe I'd like it more if I knew it was something we shared.

2. Check gauge.

Ha-ha. Um. So, this is what you're supposed to do every time you knit or crochet something new: make a small test patch with the yarn and the needles or hook the pattern calls for, so you can make sure you're getting the right number of stitches per inch and adjust accordingly, before you plunge into the thing itself and it becomes much harder to go back and correct such an overarching mistake. Some dedicated crafters will even launder their sample so they can see how it'll shrink or stretch. This doesn't matter so much when it comes to items with forgiving dimensions (blankets, bags, scarves) but in the case of fitted pieces like tops, it's crucial. And I hardly ever do it! At all! When I want to start a project, I just want to *start*, goddammit.

It'll work itself out, I think, cavalierly casting on 240 tiny stitches that will all have to be undone if it turns out that I hold the yarn tighter than the pattern's author did. And here's the thing: it usually does work out. Or at least, I've conveniently blocked out the dozens of times I've had to start over. But you should check gauge. Don't be like me. I am bad.

3. Listen to directions.

"Ugh," I say when confronted by an especially annoying pattern feature, like short-row shaping at the bust. (It's hard.) "Do I have to? I'm not going to." And then, weeks later, as the garment in question hangs down my front like an expensive silk-merino potato sack: "Damn, this pattern really should have included some short-row shaping at the bust."

4. Laundry.

I am usually much too scared to wash any of my pieces even when the yarn is specifically designed for you to do so. This means that they all smell, at best, like a sheep sheltering from the rain, and at worst like a sheep sheltering from the rain inside a locker room.

5. Neatness.

My embroideries in particular look terrible from behind. They're riddled with tangled threads, their edges haphazardly tamped down with whatever Elmer's-ass glue I happen to have on hand. I try to at least trim all the unsightly bits when a piece is meant for someone else, but if it's for me, forget it. I tell myself that there's something subversive about a craft that looks even and measured from the front and chaotic from the back; that's human nature, right? What we see on the surface has so little to do with the messy process it took to get there, and all my loose threads are a testament to that effort. They should be celebrated, not hidden! They're the real craft, the real art! But really that is just me justifying my laziness after the fact.

6. Tell my left from my right.

How often have I made a perfect, identical pair of mittens, only to realize that they are so identical that the thumbs are both on the same side? Too often, friends. Too often.

Knitting Myself
Back Together

~~~~~~

W hen I decided to move into my own apartment after
years of living with roommates, my anxiety took over
completely.

Idiot, it hissed after I signed a lease on a beautiful little place
in an unfamiliar neighborhood. *How the fuck do you think you're
ready for this? You can't afford it, it's not safe, you'll regret it, you
chose wrong.*

Before I moved, I spent six months trawling apartment-hunting
sites with perky, vague names like PadMapper and StreetEasy.
It was something like my version of porn, scrolling through
these lives I could dart into and out of as I pleased. Who would
I be if I had a patio, roof access, a shared bathroom, a dog?
How would I arrange my books and my yarn? Where did people

even buy couches, and where did you apply for the license to make such an adult decision?

I took careful notes on the average sizes of one-bedrooms and studios (shoeboxian), what I could get for my money (nearly nothing), which types of listings looked like scams (all of them). I filed away this knowledge for some far-off date, when, I expected, I would be ready and able to use it.

It was much too early to be seriously looking, especially in a city like New York where real estate moves quickly, but reading all those listings made me feel like I was doing something. Like I was building up credit that I could trade in for the life I wanted when the time was right. I could have the thrill of finding exactly what I was looking for without the commitment or the inconvenience of actually trying to get it (or, God forbid, of being disappointed by it). I liked how there usually wasn't any furniture in the listed photos to clutter my fantasies; there weren't noisy upstairs neighbors or clanging radiators, no unflushing toilets or unpaid Internet bills.

When I get there, I'd tell myself when I was annoyed with my then roommate's pile of dishes or frustrated by the people constantly streaming in and out of my then boyfriend's living room. *When I get there.*

I figured I'd be able to apply all this careful research at my leisure, that I'd surely be able to find the perfect space of my own—I'd prepared! I'd done my homework! The universe (or New York real-estate gods) practically owed it to me. But when the time kind-of-sort-of came to actually start looking, I saw only a couple of real-life apartments.

The first was located in the already-too-expensive part of Brooklyn where I lived at the time, which turned out to be in my price range only because it did not have an oven or a full-size fridge.

"I don't cook much," I reasoned to my mother over the phone. "If anything, this'll make me shop more thoughtfully!" I filled out an application because it was in a place I knew and because I was scared I wouldn't find anything else, but when the landlord called to actually interview me, I made up some weak excuse and kept searching.

The second was in another part of the city I knew because it was where Sam lived. For months I'd felt as though I lived in his apartment as much as or more than I lived in mine. (Three subway stops, five flights of stairs, and two roommates away.) My favorite clothes sat folded in neat piles on his floor, and then, when he bought a dresser, in his drawers. On the day he moved in, I sat beside him in the U-Haul. I helped carry boxes and directed his roommate in the arrangement of the couch. I silently played a game of *What if we lived here together one day?* But that never quite rose to the surface, was never something I felt safe or solid enough to want or to name. I didn't fully live anywhere: not in my house, not in his, and so I secretly, childishly hoped that finding a place of my own would solve everything.

That apartment, though, was not it. It was boxy and light-less, set on a loud and barren street, and more than anything, it just wasn't mine. I ignored the broker's follow-up texts once it became clear that everything else he wanted to show me was $400 more per month.

I decided to take a break from searching because I was making myself frantic, even with two months minus one week to go before I had to move out of my current place. What had all that work been for if I wasn't going to find my dream home immediately? Why couldn't I just *get there*?

And, of course, that's when I spotted the Craigslist post. (It was still how I unwound, even if I told myself I wasn't *looking*-looking.) I first paused my scrolling because of the unusual doorways, which were tall and open and shaped like Moroccan archways. The photographs were well lit but not staged; the place tidy but clearly lived-in. The kitchen was painted mustard yellow, which is my favorite color, and the bedroom was painted light gray, which is my favorite color to pair with mustard. It looked small but truly cozy, not "cozy" in the way New York brokers throw that word around. It looked like a home.

Even though it was fifty dollars more per month than the outer limits of my budget, and even though it was in a neighborhood I hadn't even thought to search in, within hours I was scrambling to find my most recent W-2 and my last three pay stubs. I'd shown up to the viewing and that was it—the land-lords lived directly below and were some of the kindest people I'd encountered in New York, let alone while dealing with the housing market. They were a couple with a four-year-old daughter. They complimented my sweater (I'd knitted it) and showed me their garden, where everything, they said, was either edible or medicinal and where they cooked pizzas in a large stone oven.

And the apartment itself was even homier than I'd imagined, with sweeping high ceilings and a perfect alcove for my bed. I had no trouble transposing my own furniture in place of the simple but neat belongings of the current tenants, and imagining all the new things I would get to fill out the rest: a couch for the back wall, a set of café chairs for the kitchen. When I left, my new landlords' daughter gave me a picture she'd colored of a Disney princess. I felt giddy. I'd arrived.

But almost immediately after I signed the lease, the darkly familiar rumblings started. The dreaminess of floating through all those hypothetical apartment listings turned into a hard, gnarled lump once I actually chose one. My brain turned furiously on me: what had been the point of doing all that research, all that planning, if I was just going to turn around and choose on impulse?

You did this, it said. *You were stupid and now you have nobody to blame but yourself.*

I still had six weeks to go before the move and I started to wake up every morning with my heart throwing itself against my ribs. Sam told me I had nothing to worry about, that the place seemed great; my new landlords fielded my questions about neighborhood safety and public transit options with such kindness that I felt guilty for Googling things like "lease break nyc before move in??" in the middle of the night.

Really, what all my panicked questioning translated to was this: I hated not knowing the future, not being able to chart the edges of my life and promise myself it would all be okay. I hated that I couldn't visualize exactly what my days would look like anymore. One morning I stayed home from work because I woke up to a panic attack so strong that I threw up mucus all over my sheets. I put the sheets in the bathtub of the apartment I'd soon be leaving and called my mother, who patiently repeated how great it was all going to be. Then, to stave off another wave of nausea, I began to knit a sweater.

My knitting predates my anxiety by about a decade. I'd started with doll blankets and washcloths and coasters (which all looked exactly the same) and then eventually moved on to lace cardigans, minidresses, and a lifetime supply of mismatched mittens, fueled by the impulse to make some of my shapeless fears physical.

Those more advanced projects began the summer after I graduated high school. I was unemployed and unanchored for the first time in my life, competing at the height of the economic downturn for part-time jobs at Sephora and Victoria's Secret against hot girls who had degrees in fashion merchandising. I'd decided to take the summer off from working at my beloved performing arts camp because I'd thought I should try something new, should see what a little more of the world (or at least the Natick Mall) was like before leaving for college in the fall. I wanted to see who I'd be in a new situation, not surrounded by people who'd known me my entire life; it felt like a sort of dry run before I moved three hundred miles away to a place where I would know almost nobody.

But then there was no new situation, nothing except group interviews and my parents' couch and the looming fear that whatever was coming was going to be much bigger and more jagged than what I was leaving behind. I'd been go-go-going for so long—getting good grades, getting into college, getting out of my small Massachusetts town—that when I suddenly ground to a halt, all of that percolating energy had nowhere to go.

It feels funny and far away now, that objectively tiny slice of time before I left for school. The months I would spend in this exact same state after college—trying to find a job, trying to make a home—would feel frantic but also free, nowhere near the sludgy muck of that post–high school summer. It was the first time, I guess, that I had nothing concrete to hold on to, to point at to prove that I was doing okay. I grew claustrophobic and tense, all of a sudden scared of driving and disproportionately angry (at the world, but mostly at myself) that nobody seemed to be able to see me. That chorus of *What's wrong with you, why can't you be better?* began its ragged beat, and even though I've learned to turn the volume down, it's stayed there ever since.

About a month into that summer, I pulled out my knitting needles. I'd been in a craftless phase after years spent practicing with my grandma, and at that point I'd never really gotten past that first doll-blanket-shaped endeavor. I couldn't read patterns and that alone felt like it walled me off from all the knowledge and inspiration I knew was floating around, in books and on the Internet, among people much more skilled than I who knew how to speak that secret language. I'd look at the pictures my not-quite-fellow knitters would post online and it was like looking through a thick pane of glass at something I could visualize but not touch. It was just one more way I wasn't good enough.

The difference was that I *could* get there. Knitting became my task. I started to pore over books and then YouTube videos, slowly figuring out what it meant to seam a shoulder or turn a heel. There were a lot of false starts: a pair of socks so large they looked more like a pair of casts, a horribly itchy dress with a skirt so heavy it stretched the top to twice its original length. I can't quite bring myself to throw these projects away, so they live in limbo in the closet of my childhood bedroom, feet away from where they were created. They're a reminder of how far I've come and how far I have left to go.

I knitted my very first sweater, a cropped yellow cardigan that I can't say I've ever worn, in a blurred week of near insomnia. It was a simple pattern—more of a recipe, really—that I'd had to start over three times before finally figuring out the theory. It didn't matter that the sleeves were too bulky or that the buttonholes didn't line up; here was something that was 100 percent mine, that seven days prior had been nothing but a pile of raw materials. Nobody had asked me to knit it or had given me permission. I just did it, and that power was enough to propel me into a summer of unbridled productivity. I almost forgot to be nervous when I packed up and left for school in the fall. I had, in some small way, stopped waiting to be chosen.

Still, despite finding my weapon of choice, my anxiety expanded and mutated. Sometimes it feels like its own separate person. Privately, half-jokingly, I call her Bad Alanna. She gorges herself on mistakes I make at work and feasts on fights with people I love—anything that makes it look like that happiness I've harvested, the progress I've made, could all of a sudden disappear. Bad Alanna gets furious with my past self, the one who said or did or wanted the thing in question. She feels helpless to control a given situation and that helplessness manifests as mania, as a blind rage against anything in me that she sees as broken or lacking, as a need to *do something about it* so raw that it trumps all logic.

Bad Alanna is not logical. She's all emotion, even has emotions *about* emotions—you haven't been truly upset until you're upset with yourself about being upset. And so when my good and kind brain is trying to yell above the din that *You will not be fired, he will not leave you, that had nothing to do with you so please slow your heartbeat*—I don't hear it. Or, worse, Bad Alanna hears it and gets even angrier that she can't, won't, isn't able to follow its calm directive. I have spent a lot of time trying to talk to myself and even more time straining to listen.

But making things dims the roar. The rhythm of stitches, the steadiness and solidness of the ever-growing project—those are *real*, the antidote to the made-up apocalypse that is my anxiety's favorite place to play. Crafts are under your control, progressing at (almost) exactly the rate and (usually) in exactly the manner you choose. You can't jump ahead to the finished product any more than you can fast-forward through the difficult parts, the not-knowing-what-will-come-next parts of life.

And so you have to let the process drive. Making things is a lot like yoga or sex, how it shrinks your immediate universe down to this manageable size where all you have to focus on is what's right in front of you. Unlike sex, though, at the end you get a new pair of socks or a coaster.

I can chart my roughest periods by the pile of finished and then forgotten projects nestled in the back of my old closet. There's a chunky lace shawl from my first summer in New York, the only project from when I was falling in love with Sam and out on my own for the first time. There's a pair of leg warmers from a winter break spent worrying about an art history test I'd sort of cheated on (it turned out the rest of the class had too), and the socks for Joe, my high school boyfriend, who I did not know how to firmly say goodbye to. All these pieces are imbued with a trace of energy from the time I spent working on them. They don't need to be worn. They've done their job.

In preparation for my apartment, I crafted. I finished the panic-attack sweater (another yellow cardigan I've never actually worn) and then felted a set of bowls to hold quarters for the nearby Laundromat. I couldn't find a bath mat I liked, so I knitted one with five strands of cotton yarn held together on the largest needles I owned. I embroidered quotes I liked onto little round samplers and crocheted some lacy cozies for rocks I'd collected from the beach near my parents' house.[1]

Holding these projects in my hands, watching them take shape and picturing them in my new space, made the apartment feel less abstract. I could send these tiny mercenaries out into the future and they would report back that everything would be, if not definitely okay, then at least real. And something that was real couldn't be nearly as big or formless or scary as I worried it would be. Even when I screwed up—shrank one

---

[1] This is, bar none, the thing for which my friends mock me the most: "Alanna, you made *sweaters* for *rocks*?" They have a point.

of the bowls too small, spilled red hair dye all over the white bath mat—those were problems that had solutions. Most, it turns out, do.

The moment you know you are a real knitter, for good and for keeps, is when you fix your first mistake. Before that you are a little helpless, seeking out the aid of teachers and Internet walk-throughs to take you back to the place before you made the hole, quadrupled the stitch count, yanked out the needle. That first bad summer I learned how to read my knitting, to know which loop has to be repaired in order to create the next one. To know that a lapse in attention or a jerky movement doesn't have to mean the end of anything.

So too in my non-knitting life. I am trying to learn how to trace my anxiety back to its original source so I can better understand how to face it—to prove to myself that it *can* be faced. So often the only thing you can do is give up the idea that you can perfectly visualize a life, and just keep stringing days together one by one; so often a gaping hole in a sleeve just needs a little tug a few stitches back. And sometimes you just have to sit with the hole, to accept that it's there and it's uncomfortable and it's fine.

When I moved into my new home, one of the very first things I unpacked was my yarn. It's arranged in rainbowish order on a bookshelf right across from my bed, and so when I wake up in the morning it's the first thing I see. I like having all these colors around, all that squishy, toasty goodness. I like the extravagance and the absurdity of it, that I could really only have such a display in my own solo space. More than that, though, I like the potential.

What will you be? I wonder of a large pile of marled green wool, three balls of unbleached cotton, a tiny skein of silk picked up at a festival near the college that turned out to be just right. The not-knowing isn't so bad. In fact, it could be the best part.

Things I Am Better
at Because of Crafting

1. Counting really fast* (*multiples of 5 only).

For some reason I count all my stitches in batches of five at a time, and now I do so with all other small things: playing cards, laundry quarters, any assortment of foodstuffs meant to be divided among X number of people. This is a skill that would be more impressive if everyone around me were eighteen months old, but in life you take what you are given.

2. Gripping strength.

I have a very firm and dexterous grip owing to years of clutching knitting needles as if I were locked in a permanent fencing match against myself. This makes my handshakes intimidating, or so I've been told, and I rarely have problems with jar lids.

3. Guessing other people's measurements.

Rarely when it comes to their actual bodies, but absolutely when it comes to their hands, heads, and other outcroppings. If we meet for the first time and I stare at you too long, assume that I'm calculating how much yarn would be required to swath you in knitwear.

4. Whining about how expensive commercially manufactured garments are.

"Urban Outfitters is charging *how much* for this and it's made of *acrylic*? Shit is *flammable*. I could crochet this out of *merino wool* in, like, *two hours* for *one-third of the cost* and it would last long enough to *give to your goddamn grandchildren*. Wait, Moriah, where are you going? Put that back."

5. Untying knots.

Once you've had to face down a tangled skein of lace-weight silk that was too expensive to even consider cutting, you can overcome even the most stubborn shoelaces or headphone cords.

Body Talk

Bodies are the worst. They make smells and noises when you least want them to. They're too big in some parts and too small in others (sometimes, bafflingly, in the same exact parts) and they host a buffet of aches, pains, sores, and general creaks. They break down and they break out.

They betray. They invite unwanted people and comments and judgments; they stand for who you are in a way that can feel so grossly inaccurate. *Why can't I just be that brain in a vat?* you wonder on certain hungover mornings, trying to squeeze into a pair of pants that fit just fine last week but now sit in such a way as to frame that tummy roll that never used to be there in college, or maybe you just didn't used to care.

Bodies are the best. They help you get where you want to go, and then sometimes when you arrive you can use them to sing or dance or have sex. When you least expect them to, they take over from your stupid loud brain. *You can do this*, they say in a voice far deeper and calmer than your own. *You are more than this moment right here.* Some of them can literally create new people! They operate in a thousand ways you can never fully understand, carrying you and swaddling you even when they are frustrating. Sometimes they let you down far too early; sometimes they chug along until it's time.

"I can't imagine living to ninety," my grandma said on her last Christmas. "How many days do you have to brush your damn teeth?"

Bodies just . . . are. They're sites of pain and pleasure, meaning and misunderstanding, deeply personal, deeply public, with you and against you and totally unconcerned with you. What they all require, at least where I live, is clothes. As if it's not hard enough just to *have* a body, now you have to *buy* things to *put* on it in order to take it out with you into the world. You have to listen as you're told, again and again, that you aren't quite right, that you aren't quite *real*, just because you can't always pour your glorious whole self into an arbitrary series of fabric tubes (made by someone living on the same planet in the same year as you but who most likely isn't making close to a living wage, designed and peddled and delivered to you by a faceless corporation that has no interest in your humanity be-sides the Red Sox debit card sitting in your falling-apart wallet, a corporation that does, in fact, benefit from your continued sense of incompletion).

I actually do like clothes, and for the most part I have the sort of body I've been taught deserves to wear them: white, thin, cisgender, from a comfortable background and a comfortable life. I can't begin to imagine the struggles of people who have to contend with a society that yells far worse epithets than *"Huge schnoz!"* or *"It's amazing how you manage to rock both acne and wrinkles at the same time, Benjamin fucking Button!"* (That one is courtesy of my own brain.)

Largely, I like the way I look. I like my shoulders, straight from years of choir posture, and my smile, even though it crinkles my eyes down to nothing in photographs. I like that my boobs are sort of small and my butt is sort of big; I even like my nose and eyebrows (both at least a size too large), which inspired mean enough comments to make me cry when I was younger. I like wearing fancy jumpsuits and crop tops, and winged eyeliner, and lots of earrings. I like doing my makeup every morning, those ten or fifteen minutes of confronting my own face and smoothing it out. I like arming myself gently, softly, against the onslaught of being in the world.

But I do still hear the ways in which I fall short, because I am not a brain in a vat. I hear them from boys and from girls, and from ads on the subway and shows on HBO and most of all from myself. I hear them whispered by my dimpled thighs and hissed by the flaps under my upper arms. I hear them emanate from dressing-room mirrors, where I've brought in ten items and can't find a single one that doesn't make my lower half look, to me, cartoonishly outsize.

"You could wear a paper bag and still look great," my mom has told me throughout my life. I appreciate this more than I could ever say but it can be hard to hear clearly once the cacophony gets too loud. And for as long as she's been telling me that, it seems, she's been putting down her own body, even though she is the kind of beautiful I can't wait to be.

"I'll buy this when I lose ten pounds," she says, almost as often as she reassures me. I don't see where these ten pounds lurk, but I know that she does.

What do you do when you figure out the world isn't made for you? Remake it yourself so that it fits. Or, at least, so that a small corner of it does. I was overwhelmed when I first started considering knitting projects larger than scarves, more involved than hats; every pattern I read stressed the importance of measuring, of checking the yarn's gauge but also knowing exactly how many inches you were at your various parts. I'd adopted a sort of don't-ask-don't-tell policy when it came to my physical self. I knew how much I weighed, vaguely, but didn't like to look at scales. I once told a friend that I sometimes liked to forget that I had a body, except as a receptacle to put Kit Kats in.

But once I started knitting and crocheting for myself I had to look head-on, or else risk a garment that either wouldn't make it past my shoulders or would turn out too large to stuff under my winter coat.

The first time I really measured myself, I was seventeen or eighteen years old. I'd found a pattern for a simple pullover sweater with a floppy cowl neck, and bought purple silk-merino yarn that cost significantly more than it would have to buy the same sweater at the mall. It was straightforward knitting and meant to hang loose, with plenty of room for forgiveness on both the technical and physical sides, but still required that I stand in front of my bedroom mirror and wrap a tape measure around my chest, my waist, and my hips.

I stopped thinking, for a moment, about my body as anything other than the vehicle for this beautiful item I wanted so badly to bring into the world. I stopped thinking that it had to look or be anything other than what it was, because the sweater, somehow, would conform to its requests. My body had nothing to do just then with sex, food, pain, worthiness, or value. It was just there, and it was mine, and so too would be this sweater.

The type of pattern I picked was called a top-down raglan, which a decade later is still my favorite construction. You start at the neck and work your way down and outward, making a sort of chest plate–looking piece of fabric that is eventually divided into sections for your arms and torso. It looks distinctly unsweaterlike for a long time, but the real appeal is that you get to try it on as you go. If you decide you want your armholes looser or your neckline longer, you can make tweaks without needing to start over. (The alternatives, among which are sweaters knitted from the bottom up and in pieces that need to be sewn together at the end, are much less charitable.)

So that's what I did. For three weeks I knitted, wriggling in and out of the sweater in front of that same mirror, making adjustments when I found that it was much too wide around the bust (typical) and when I decided I wanted it to be more cropped (also typical). When it was finished, there was almost no extra work to be done, just a few armpit stitches to graft together and some loose ends to trim.

I tried it on. Even though I'd known it would fit—that was basically the whole point of the exercise—when I popped my head through the neck hole and saw how it skimmed over my body, I was surprised. I guess I'd just expected something to go wrong, that either my knitting wouldn't be up to par or I wouldn't. Or worse, that it would be kinda-sorta right, one more item that walked like a sweater and quacked like a sweater but wasn't *quite* a sweater, nothing I would want to wear beyond the threshold of my bedroom.

But this? This looked like a real sweater. And I was the real, solid, complete person who had made it.

There is such power in creating something designed to fit only you. It's a quiet fuck-you to any clothing company or magazine or person that's ever made you feel less. I branched out into more-fitted clothes—tank tops, dresses, an extremely ill-advised pair of shorts—all of which required me to learn my circumferences, my lengths, and my preferences. I started to copy the drapey openwork sweaters at Anthropologie and the lacy crop tops at Free People, and to add little touches of my own: a knitted hem, a breast pocket. I created new patterns entirely; one sweater I made up as I went, switching between five variations of a particular reddish yarn according to however I was feeling at that moment. I learned that I am "short waisted," whatever that means, and so, therefore, is every garment I've ever made. That's just how they are, the way they're supposed to be. Their job is to fit me, and so they do. I wish that was how I'd been trained to feel about all clothes, that I wasn't so constantly barraged with the worry that I was the one who didn't fit right.

Of course crafting isn't a cure-all for the poisons that seep in everywhere. So many patterns don't include enough sizes; knitwear models are still models, and therefore all too often young and thin and white, not at all reflective of the range of people seeking to make things for themselves.[1] Materials are expensive, and lessons are time-consuming and not always accessible. I try to be aware of where the yarn I buy comes from, to know that the people and animals involved in its production are being

---

[1] Probably the first article I wrote that I was really proud of was an investigation into a phenomenon that the knitting community had long been aware of but that had escaped the attention of the greater populace: former *America's Next Top Model* contestants pose for knitting magazines in *droves*. It's like there's a funnel from the judging room to the casting couch at *Vogue Knitting*.

treated fairly, but I know that I slip. I get lazy; I get enticed by a sweater's-worth of acrylic that's almost definitely made from the same stuff as a tire. It's the way I am at the grocery store, where cage-free eggs sound great but don't ever quite seem to make it into my basket when the other, presumably cage-full option is right there and $2 cheaper.

Besides, "Just make your own clothes!" doesn't solve any of the central issues: the way bodies are sized up and accepted or dismissed on sight, the way we're taught to turn our hatred inward, all the ways we are shown again and again that we're nothing but a collection of problems to be solved. Crafting doesn't exempt you from the confines of capitalism—you're still the one buying, spending, investing, hustling. If anything, it's a moment of suspension, an exception that proves the relentless and insidious rule.

But it can help. It can remind you, however briefly, that you're not fully at the mercy of the gears that threaten to grind you up. "Look what I made" isn't just a cute little mewl for attention; it can be a battle cry. "Look." It can be a command. "Look at me, as I am, as I want to be. I did this. I made this, and you can't ever take it away."

Handmade clothes get a bad rap. They're often the punch lines in Not Just for Grandmas™ moments: the itchy, horrible sweater that the recently dumped roommate knits in between bites of Ben & Jerry's, the crocheted vest that the art teacher wears every day of the school year without knowing the mocking names that the boys at the back of the class call both it and her. (Don't even get me started on Ugly Sweater parties.) These clothes are unwanted, they're unlovable, they're awkward and earnest and show a certain delusion on the part of their creator. *There are already plenty of clothes in the world*, these portrayals argue; *who asked you to bring in more? Sit down and be quiet.*

This premise is flawed in too many ways to count, not least of which is that (a) crocheted vests are dope and I wish I had one and (b) there are limitless cute/cool/strange/slutty/cozy patterns out there, plus an extra infinity in the minds of people who don't work from patterns at all. And contained in this critique is, again, the tacit idea that clothes (and food and homes and so many other things that fall under the nebulous banner/ market category of "lifestyle") are frivolous, something that should be beneath concern for anyone who's smart or important or serious. And, yeah, nobody's going to knit the cure for cancer, but nobody's going to score a touchdown that cures cancer either.

I always used to hate the idea of "expressing yourself"; for some reason it reminded me of, like, little kids on the Disney Channel wearing red-tinted sunglasses and dancing on a giant keyboard, this loud and garish assertion of Self that didn't actually have much to do with the slippery core of you. But I realize that's what I'm arguing for here, what I fight for every time I decide to put something new in the world, every day that I opt to wear something that I saw through from idea to materials to completion. I *want* people to ask me about my sweaters and tank tops; I want them to know that's the sort of person I am, that I have this extremely minor superpower even if they think it's weird or dorky. This is how I choose to spend my time and my brain space, and I want my physical being to reflect that, at least every once in a while.[2] It feels like a better use for my body, at any rate, than just as something to lug around and resent.

And look: it's not that serious. You don't have to wage a war every time you choose a ball of yarn, and you certainly don't have to love something just because someone made it. (This goes double if it's a hand-me-down.) Or even if *you* made it. I've knitted so many ugly sweaters! And not because I was going to some stupid Christmas party! The gap between expectation and execution gets in the way, or I run out of steam halfway or sometimes 95 percent of the way through, or it turns out that there is approximately one a day per year when the weather is suitable for a wool-blend crop top. I don't think these pieces are politically useful art or even that anyone should ever want to wear them, let alone me.

But I'm so glad I took the time to make them, that I dreamed up a new idea or saw a picture of a girl in a lacy tank top or an off-the-shoulder sweater and thought, *Hey, I could pull that off.* And that I *did* pull it off, in both senses. I have this insane fantasy of knitting my own wedding dress to my exact specifi-

---

[2] In one of my worst and most me moments in recent history, I whined to Aude that the cardigan I'd just finished knitting was too good, and so people just assumed I'd bought it. She snorted at me, as well she should have.

cations, of making hats for my future babies and the babies of everyone I love, of covering every inch of my home, wherever that may be, in needlepoint samplers and crocheted floor poufs and blankets that only exist because I decided that they should. I want to make the whole world, but that gets so daunting. And so I start with me.

Words They Need to Invent for Crafters

~~~~~~~~~~~~~~~~~~~~~~~~~~~~~~

1. The paralysis that kicks in when you have such beautiful yarn or fabric that you're scared to start making something, because what if you can't do it justice?

2. The proud but irritating moment when a project becomes too big/heavy/precious to take anywhere, and so the only place you can work on it is at home.

3. When you make a "typo" in an embroidery and only realize once it's too late.

4. The blood-boiling rage of reaching an especially fiddly part of a project and then the phone rings or somebody starts to talk to you.

5. The blood-boiling rage of someone you don't know or like very well asking, however jokingly, if you will make them something.

6. The blood-boiling rage of being told that crafters are supposed to be a calm bunch and therefore should not experience blood-boiling rage.

7. That tiny little mistake you know that nobody else will ever notice but that you can't look away from.

8. The suffocating silence at the end of the podcast or audiobook you were crafting alongside for hours or weeks.

9. When you lose a sewing needle in your bed and can't find it, but you know it's there, lurking, waiting to stab you when you least expect it.

Second Sock Syndrome

W hat happens," a friend once asked me, "when you finish one sock and *do not want* to knit the other?"

She had knitted one of a white-and-blue pair and was too annoyed to go on to the next. She thought it was lumpy and ugly,
didn't like how the colors of the yarn had pooled rather than
striped. I suggested that she punch through and just make the
second one anyway, because having a pair would be better than
having just one, and also why not? But we both knew that sock
was going to remain the only one of its kind.

Like the Curse of the Boyfriend Sweater, this is a common
enough condition to have a name (although a far less sexy one):
Second Sock Syndrome. It can afflict any knitter regardless of

skill level, and any would-be pair of socks, even ones that aren't a disappointment. Occasionally it strikes mittens, leg warmers, booties, or other twosomes, but it rears its head overwhelmingly in the presence of socks.

This epidemic is partly due to the fact that making even just one sock is *hard*. They're my all-time favorite project to knit, portable and customizable and with enough distinct stages to keep it interesting, but I can only manage a pair every half a year or so without succumbing to sock fatigue. (Not to mention the fact that they're ridiculously difficult to care for if you don't use yarn that can be put through a washing machine; it's fine to hand-wash a cardigan every now and then, but foot stink is tough to scrub out.)

And the other part, I suspect, is that socks have a sort of mythic quality: it's hard to believe that they can be made in the first place. They're such a quotidian object that it seems more likely for them to grow on vines somewhere or be chipped from the walls of a mine. But they're also the quintessential knitted item, immortalized in the hands of cartoon spinsters and requested by even the most remote strangers—"Ooh, will you make me socks?"—within minutes of finding out you are, in fact, a knitter. I knew I was a boring, terrible adult the year I started requesting expensive woolen socks for Christmas and Hanukkah (you can't make them *all* yourself). Eight-year-old Alanna would be furious with me.

~~~

Here is how you make a sock. You can begin knitting from either direction, the toe or the leg opening. I tend to go for the latter, because it's how I first learned, but toe-up is generally regarded as the best way—if you run out of yarn, you can just make the sock shorter in the cuff, instead of starting over or switching to a different yarn. But I like to live on the edge.

Because the yarn and needles are so tiny (more like dental floss and toothpicks), you generally have to cast on an improbable number of stitches for an adult-sized sock.

Seventy-two?! I remember thinking early on in my sock-knitting career. *But that's how many you need for a hat!* It's all in the yarn bulk. You could use thick, cushy yarn to make your sock, but as I've experienced, it would turn out to more closely resemble a cast.

So there you are with your many dozens of eensy-weensy stitches, and, insult to injury, far more needles than you were ever told by popular culture you'd be expected to knit with. Because socks, and most small-circumferenced tubular items, are knitted on lethal-looking double-pointed needles, or DPNs.[1] Watching someone knit with four or five needles at once is especially fascinating to people in public places, like the subway; they will tap you on the shoulder or even ask you to remove your headphones in order to ask what you are doing. You will

---

[1] There's a method that involves one long circular needle called, fittingly, the Magic Loop; there's also a way to knit two socks at a time, which solves this whole problem in one go. But I've never really mastered either technique, the same way I've never really learned how to hold the yarn, and sort of enjoy the masochistic struggle.

get to feel equal parts smug and annoyed by this interruption, and then you will probably drop a stitch.

Immediately after the cast-on comes the cuff. Cuffs are the unsung heroes of the fiber world. They're elastic and forgiving, stretching to accommodate the flippers you never knew your roommate was concealing inside his Converses and shrinking to keep a new baby's doll-sized ankle warm. Cuffs are a joy to knit, repetitive and quick, and each time I make one I entertain the possibility of going rogue and turning the project into something totally different than I'd planned. *Thought you were gonna be a sock? Well, now you're a sweater sleeve and I am the master of the universe!*

(I have never actually done that.)

After the cuff is the leg, simple and straightforward. It's like driving along a flat highway at sundown. And like a highway, it can lull you into a false sense of security—"Look at me, I'm knitting a sock!"—because right after that comes the heel. The heel is what scares people, and with good reason. If you think about feet long enough, which knitting a sock requires you to do, you start to realize what a strange part of the already-strange human body they are, all bones and tapers and right angles. And a knitted object is, at its heart, a tiny feat of engineering designed to contain all that strangeness. It's a series of problems solved in sequence. A lot of these problems are easy: how do I connect this loop to the one before, after, atop, and below? They can be holistic: how do I cover this body part/household object/dog with a piece of fabric that makes the most sense, that doesn't add too much bulk, that still allows it to complete its necessary tasks, like pouring tea or breathing? Knitting would be much easier if we all decided to just shove our extremities into unconnected tubes—no more shoulder seaming! Not a bust dart in sight! But we haven't yet written that addendum into the social contract, and so sometimes the problem in question has another layer, or requires (horror of horrors) *math*. That is the heel of a sock.

A heel acts as a hinge of sorts, the spot where you go from knitting vertically (the leg) to horizontally (the foot). You generally accomplish this with a fiddly technique called short-row shaping, which requires you to turn around before the end of a row and backtrack, over and over again, according to some simple but not always intuitive arithmetic. It's the opposite of, or at least perpendicular to, what you're supposed to do in knitting—move ever forward, no matter what snag you hit— and it's daunting enough to repel the most seasoned crafters.

Oh, but once you get it down, that's some real master-of-the-universe shit right there. You don't knit a heel so much as you conquer it, and once you're finally on the other side the rest of the sock feels like an easy slide to the finish, nothing but gradual decreases until the toe. You seam it up and weave in the excess pieces of yarn. You exhale. Maybe you even try it on. And then you remember: you have to make another. You despair.

~~~~

When you finish the last row of something, you just straight-up want to be *done*. It's the same instinct that often keeps me from sewing up mere inches of fabric or trimming the edges of embroideries, that keeps me leaving loose yarn ends dangling for months, the projects trapped in unwearable limbo. There's a basket of these almost-but-not-quite objects at the foot of my bed and finishing them all would probably require no more than an hour of work in total. But then, I never want to do the little work, so impatient to reach the end that I jump ahead to the next project without making time to nudge the first over the finish line. (Refer back to "The Curse of the Boyfriend Sweater" for further details.)

There are actually services that will do your finishing work for you, but the next best thing is to do it yourself while drunk. Then it's like a kindly elf did it for you in the night. It only works at a certain level of intoxication—the same two beers that impel me to do all the dishes and scrub down the bathtub— or else you run the risk of accidentally cutting an important stitch and watching all your work unravel before your tipsy eyes.

Making a second sock can feel like all the seaming in the world, only worse.

Isn't this enough? you want to shout when you hold the completed thing in your hand. *Whose idea was it to make us so symmetrical?*

While the Curse of the Boyfriend Sweater is about your relationship with someone else—your expectations, your disappointments, your hopes all tangled up together—Second Sock Syndrome is entirely about and within you. It's not *that* hard to make two of something. Remember when you had to write valentines for every kid in your kindergarten class? Remember last weekend, when you made two and a half sandwiches and ate them all while standing over your kitchen sink? You do the same things practically every day—wake up, go to work, go home, have a drink, watch your show, fall asleep—so why now this aversion to repetition?

Two theories, both bearing equal weight:

1. What people get wrong about crafting is that it's not exactly about calm and quiet. Yes, it slows you down, but what I love most about it is how this miniature propulsive force kicks in. I spend so much time launching into some imagined, uncertain future months ahead of myself, or else dwelling days behind on something I said or did (or something I should have said or done). With crafting, you're still looking ahead, but only as far as your hands; you still look back, but only to see how far you've come already.

   Having to make two of something disrupts that nowness. Making *more* is actually fine—say, forty squares to be sewn together for a blanket—because it changes the atomic unit of the project. Instead of rows, you can track your progress in squares completed. But two is too few units. No matter how firmly you tell your brain not to celebrate, that one sock is only half of the eventual whole, it doesn't want to listen. And then the disappointment of having to pull out those tiny needles all over again is that much more acute. It feels more like déjà vu than progress—shouldn't you be past the leg by now, past the cuff, certainly past the heel? What are you learning from doing the same thing over and over again? How will you ever move forward?

2. It's really fucking boring.

But there are a few solutions. One is to always have a couple of projects going on at the same time, in a couple different weights of yarn: one very bulky to provide instant gratification, like a chunky cowl; one medium and long-term, like a sweater or an afghan; and the socks in question. When you're bored of one, you can always pick up the other for a while. It's a little like adjusting the focus on a pair of binoculars.

It can also help if they are not for you; gift socks, I've found, are easier to slog through because there's an identifiable goal, some amount of gratitude waiting at the other end. No matter how wonderful hand-knit socks you made yourself can be, they're even better when they're made by someone you love. Gifts also presumably have some sort of deadline, a holiday or a birthday or a bribe, which keeps the second sock from languishing forever.

And the best tip I can offer, to knitters and non-knitters alike, is that socks don't actually have to match. Society just tells you that they should.

Things I've Used
Knitting Needles for
Besides Knitting

1. Surreptitiously picking my teeth.
2. Very obviously picking my teeth.
3. Reaching between the kitchen counter and the oven, where I had dropped a chip. I did not eat the chip after its rescue, which I think entitles me to some sort of adulthood merit badge.
4. Scratching my leg when the person I was dating at the time got bedbugs. I knew that scratching would only make the bites worse, but somehow rationalized that if I used a separate implement instead of my own nails, it was okay.
5. Putting my hair in a bun.
6. Removing the foil from the top of a wine bottle.
7. Testing to see if a cake is done.

8. Arranging in various receptacles throughout my apartment, sort of as decorations, sort of as totems, never organized such that I can find the right quantity of the right size when I actually need them.

9. Fake dueling.

10. Fake wand-waving.

11. Gripping in my fist while walking home alone once or twice. I don't know if I could *really* bring myself to do something drastic, because luckily I've never had to. Nothing ever worse than aggressive catcalls and a few guys who've followed me for a block or two before losing interest, but even that is enough to make me run-walk to my door and sit slumped on the hall carpet, willing my heart to slow back down. When I was younger I loved this book called *The Secret of Platform 13*, sort of a cousin of/precursor to the Harry Potter universe. I don't recall any plot points except that one of the villains kills people by stabbing them through the soft part of their temples with a knitting needle. I think about that almost every time I knit.

Bad Habits

I don't let people look at the pictures on my phone. Lots of folks are like this; the average photo roll is an embarrassing repository of rejected selfie drafts and grainy nudes, mixed in among images of family pets moving too fast to capture and the labels of wine bottles that will never be sought to buy.

I've taken only a handful of naked pictures in my life and I tend to delete my thousands of low-quality multiples in cleaning fits on the subway. But I've never erased a certain type of photo that pops up again and again as I scroll past months of images: the top back of my head, neck bent forward, showing a startling and ever-growing patch of white skin beneath my reddish hair. I started taking the pictures in an attempt to stop myself from pulling out the hairs one by one, but after a while they became more of a passive documentation as the bald spot grew ever bigger.

"I'll find it," I say, grabbing back my phone when a friend tries to find a photo of my family's dog or a coworker asks to approve a group shot. "Just one sec."

In general I fuss. I'm a nail biter as well as a hair puller, a pore squeezer, and a ruthless tweezer of brow and chin and nipple hairs. Never sitting still, never allowing myself to just be; often I feel like my body isn't a static, whole thing, but a collection of tiny pieces to be tended and tamed. Finding a split end to peel apart or a hangnail to pull at gives me a grim kind of jolt. It's a task I can complete, a false but momentarily satisfying way of lurching closer to—what? Perfection? Smoothness? Some time or space where I don't need to pick anymore, where I can dust off my hands and say, *There, good, done?*

Whatever it is, I do it relentlessly: at work, on the train, sitting alone in my house. My brain always wants something to fixate on, and my body is always within reach.

The nail biting is as old as my memory. I started when I was a child, as soon as I realized that nose picking was not a sustainable public option. Whenever a nail is long enough to start showing that white half-moon sliver at the top, I go for it, like a gardener who can tell when the tomatoes or basil are perfectly in season. Sometimes I bite at nails that are barely there at all, working my teeth underneath the smallest possible edge. I try to maneuver so that I leave a clean, continuous line, but sometimes I miscalculate and rip up too much, leaving the remaining nail split or jagged.

Sometimes there is blood. Blood isn't good; it means that I wasn't methodical enough. Pain of any kind, in any of my countless little pick-pick-pickings, isn't the goal—I want to fix, after all, not harm—but it does make me alert, like I am alive in the world. If I hurt, I am having an effect. If I leave a mark, I was there. The pain you bring on yourself is comforting, in a way, a means of beating your anxiety or your heartbreak or your restlessness to the punch: at least you're in control of this small thing. And ultimately, it's never been painful enough to keep me from going back for more.

I know this is bad. I know I should quit. Nail biting in particular is such a young, frantic thing to do, especially when you are trying to come across as a semi-responsible almost-adult making her way through the world. From a foot away my nails look short but otherwise respectable—"I keep them like this for knitting purposes!" I've lied before, answering a question that nobody's ever actually asked. It's only when you examine them up close that you see the unmistakable waviness, the ripped-up cuticles. Every now and then I buy a nail file and some nice polish in an attempt to shield my fingers from my own teeth. But eventually, inevitably, I peel the polish off in strips, and it litters the carpet beneath my desk like sad confetti. I do not get manicures, because I'm embarrassed by the state of my stubs. Not long ago, an old woman hissed, "Disgusting!" to me as I chomped while waiting at a crosswalk. I can't say I blame her.

The hair pulling is new. Two or three years ago I started noticing these dry, curly little hairs ringing my otherwise straight part, and so I would tug them out, I told myself, in the interest of combatting frizz and letting better ones grow in. They didn't, of course, but I learned that I liked the hunt. Nails are limited—you either have enough new growth in ten possible spots or you don't—but there could always be a bad hair lurking somewhere on your head. In fact, they're more likely to crop up in the spot you just tore from a few days ago (new hairs are usually coarse and spiky, easy to identify by feel among the soft rest of it) and so my right hand learned to gravitate toward that now-well-documented place at the top back of my skull.

I tried to only pull one hair at a time and I liked to examine it afterward. The darker and drier and more tightly corkscrewed, the better, because it meant that this ugly thing was no longer a part of me. Sometimes I'd look down at the bright-white surface of my desk and my stomach would twist at the sight of a few stray hairs. I preferred to think that once I ripped them out, they would evaporate.

The first time I quit was about a year in. A coworker took some photos of me for an article he was writing about a new app, including one from behind and slightly above. When it was published, all I could see was the jagged white spot that pooled at the end of my part. Probably nobody else ever noticed, but it repulsed me. I hated seeing that vulnerable patch of skull peeking through my hair, hated that it was public, and so I stopped pulling. I just stopped—family lore claims that I quit sucking my thumb cold-turkey the night before starting kindergarten and never relapsed—and for a few months, that was it. I kept up the biting and the picking but my hands stopped floating up to the top of my head except to occasionally pat the new growth. In a few photos from that time you can see a funny little tuft, too short to lie flat but longer than I'd ever before allowed it to grow. My sudden stoppage was like losing the taste for a certain food: I missed pulling in the same way I now miss Happy Meals—abstractly, nostalgically, with no real desire to actually seek one out.

But then I did miss it. I'd stopped in the winter and by summer, for seemingly no reason other than the low-grade anxiety that always percolates, I'd started scanning the surface of my head again. I found one irresistibly yankable hair and then another and soon enough there was a patch of raw skin even larger than the one I'd cultivated the first time.

I learned there was a name for this condition from an article written by another colleague—"trichotillomania," which sounds so haunting and Victorian—and that it overwhelmingly affects young women. There are as many as 15 million people in the United States who have it. I could never quite decide if knowing its name and stats made me feel better or worse. Did it mean that I was part of something bigger than me and therefore not alone? That I was legible, and therefore fixable? Or did it mean that I was predictable, just one more nervous girl with an imaginary problem she created but couldn't put a stop to? In some small, sick way I liked to think that I discovered this, that I was the first to have such a strong instinct to grab and twist and control that I invented a new means of harvesting from my own self. But no, there is nothing new here, just the same mechanical impulse that governs millions of other bodies.

I started snapping my own photos the second time around, hoping I could recapture the repulsion that made me stop before. But maybe it was the initial shock that had done it then, or maybe it was the fact that someone else, however unknowingly, had been the one to take the picture. Whatever it was, I couldn't seem to get it back. It looked startling, my gallery of bald patches, but it was somehow flattened in the photos, easier to divorce from reality. Did the backs of other people's heads look like this? I would wonder, making mental notes of part-width and hair distribution. Did other people spend this much time biting and tugging at themselves? If they all did, how would we ever get anything done?

It does not take years of therapy to notice that these same repetitive impulses crop up in other places. I pick at my heart in the same way as my nail beds. I replay conversations with boys over and over again, trying to pinpoint exactly where I fucked up, said too much, could have been less or more or better. I click through Instagram profiles and Twitter feeds with an obsessive automation that should land me in jail: has the person I'm dating posted something since the last time I texted them, proving that they're alive and available but just ignoring me? Have they been exchanging too many messages with someone else, or liking their photos in an especially lascivious way? I can't begin to see into another person in all their chaotic unknowability but I can read text laid out on a screen, and so I refresh and revisit as if I'm looking for understanding when I know all I will ever get are those sharp pricks of pain.

Stop hitting yourself, says the cartoon bully who is me. *Stop hitting yourself.*

That is the most frustrating part: performing the same exhaustive motion over and over again while knowing full well that nothing will be different. Like watching yourself in a horror movie, screaming helplessly at tiny on-screen you not to open that fucking door. If you are looking for proof that someone doesn't want you or that you don't matter, you will find it; most of the time you can even manufacture it yourself. If you are looking for a piece of skin or a hair to rip, one will always turn up. I spend so much time and energy picking at myself that I worry one day there will be nothing left.

My obsessive picking has no antidote but it does have a good twin. Crafting lives in the same part of my brain (maybe right underneath the ever-expanding bald patch). It's also a version of that desire to control my immediate surroundings—not through destruction, but through creation. The mechanical growling inside me that calls for a hair or a sliver of nail is also sated, temporarily, by a stitch. For a while I kept a knitting or embroidery project by my desk at work, and when my hand would start its journey toward the top of my head, I'd force it toward the craft instead. All it took was a couple of purls, a single letter of a stitched word, and the machine would be diverted.

But then it would start back up again, and maybe I didn't have a project or maybe the extra ounce of effort was just too much, and I would pull. It felt like paralysis even though I was in motion. The same way I fall into holes of not writing, not working out, not doing chores, even though I feel so good when I do those things and so bad when I don't, even when the distance between the doing and the not is the width of a hair.

Why can't you stop?

Pluck.

Why can't you stop?

Nibble.

Why can't you start?

Blank page, dirty laundry, unsent email: these things call out to be done and when I just can't make myself, they tut and tsk. Pulled hair, sliver of nail, strip of skin torn from the side of a cuticle: they whisper that I'm not good enough, that I'm lazy and weak and will never be able to control anything. They're probably right about this last one.

Crafting replicates the motion of productivity without the pressure. Sweaters don't call out to be knitted even when they've been lying in half-finished limbo for months. Or if they do, it's at least a plaintive, gentle cry. They don't stew or mutate in their undoneness, becoming scarier the longer they're put off, like those other tasks. They don't grow to monstrous heights the second they are left alone for too long, becoming symbols of your inefficiency, signs that you've been faking it the whole time. Crafts stay the same, patient, exactly the size that they are until such time as they become larger. Nobody asked for them to be made except me, and I know they'll get done. I can reach out and touch the thousands of hours of proof in my closet and on my walls. Sometimes it feels like the only thing I am sure of is this.

But you can't knit forever. You can bring it on the subway and even into some of the more chill work environments, but at some point the movement has to find its way into your fingers and stay. That's what I was hoping for when I tried to replace the hair pulling: that crafting's calm power would linger and save me. That's what I hope for, even if I don't name it, every time I pull out an incomplete embroidery sampler or a half-crocheted scarf.

Make me better, I ask of it.

Or, no: *Take me back to myself.*

One day, maybe, the hairs will not grow back. I'll reach up to grab one and find nothing but rawness. And isn't that in some twisted, backward way what I want? To reach a point of smoothness, blankness, with nothing left to complete? Every now and then I look down at one of my projects and find a single hair, caught in the yarn or thread, suddenly a part of the fabric. It mars but also strangely enhances, adds a glint of light, a disruption. I try to pull these hairs out when I find them but often they snap, woven in too tightly to slide out on their own.

Just like my habits are cyclical, so is the stopping. I quit hair pulling again about a year after the first time and, for the most part, haven't started back up. I went to see my beloved hairdresser, Vanessa, after a month spent pulling so consistently that I was starting to notice the patch when I leaned my head forward, even without the aid of a phone or a mirror. That was never the plan—I liked to have it out of my sight, only visible when mediated, when I chose to see it. I was long overdue for a cut and color but hated the thought of someone spending time so close to my scalp. Still, the appointment was hard to schedule because she was so in demand, so I parted my hair on the opposite side and went.

Vanessa hugged me hello, asked me how work was going. I sat down in her chair and faced the mirror. She ran her fingers through my limp, dry hair, and just as I was about to explain away the bald patch, she said, "So you're still pulling, huh?"

Of course she'd noticed before; I'd been going to her the entire time. But we'd never spoken about it and so I figured it was just one of those pleasant half lies you exchange, like telling the doctor you have half as many drinks and twice as many hours of exercise per week as you actually do.

"Yeah," I admitted. "It's gotten pretty bad."

"I have a friend who used to do this. You should stop."

I was irritated by this—of course I should stop! Didn't she think I was trying? I wanted so badly to swat her hand out of the way and pull a hair or two, just to have some way to channel my frustration, but instead I let her wash it and dye it and chop it into the short, layered cut that only she could ever make look good on me.

"Remember about the pulling!" she said as I left.

Yeah, okay, I thought.

But I went home, and I didn't pull. At first it was because Vanessa had blown out my hair so smooth that I couldn't find a bad one worthy of ripping out. Then it was because I hadn't done it the day before, or the day before that. I have an app on my phone where I track how often I exercise (rarely) and write (all the time or not at all) and floss (haaaa), and I made a new entry: Didn't Pull. That one, I've kept up. Each night, right before bed, I swipe the task to show that it's been completed. It keeps track of the days, and before I knew it I'd hit a streak of 100, and then 101, and then 102 and beyond. It turns out that not pulling, when measured like the ever-repeating stitches of a scarf, brings me almost the same satisfaction as pulling, at least for right now. There is still a lifetime of days to go, but for today I am happy with my little scrap.

An Open Letter
to Crochet

~~~~~~

Dear Crochet,

We both know that knitting is my first love. I don't need to tell you how it's been there for me since before I could read: smooth and consistent, steady and loyal. I can usually even do it without looking.

But sometimes, Crochet, you're all that I crave. I don't even remember how you came into my life—the Internet? Some night when I had too much to drink? My grandma, probably?—but since then you've added a dimension I just can't live without. I love how textured and open you are (knitting can be so stiff!) and how appealingly flexible. Knitting requires working all of those stitches at once, and if you drop one, game over. You, on the other hand, don't ask for much—just a single stitch worked at a time, so I can switch directions at a moment's notice. I can't tell you how liberating it feels to know that I can change my mind as I go with you, even if I'm usually too scared and straitlaced to take the plunge.

You let me express myself. If I want to make a star or a flower or an anatomically correct human heart, it's you I'll always turn to. You have the soul of an artist.

It hasn't always been easy. You're temperamental and untrustworthy—what the hell happens to all those stitches at the beginnings of rows? I'm certainly not skipping them! And you go through yarn like a maniac; sometimes I think you take up twice as much as knitting does, for basically the same results. I have to watch you at all times to make sure I'm not getting tangled up, and even though I'm a strong, confident woman, you've managed to gaslight me into thinking I was wrong when I totally wasn't.

But through it all, sometimes I just plain want you. You know what I think it is? With knitting, I always have to wait for an aha moment, when the thing I've been making finally starts to resemble what it really is. But you, Crochet, never pretend to be something you're not. And for that, you'll always have your hooks in me.

With yarn and yearning,

Alanna

Fiberspace

~~~~~~

It feels like a lie by omission to have gone this far without really mentioning the Internet. Because at this point I live online about as much as I live in my apartment, and probably get a lot more done in the former.

Partly this is because of my job. I worked for a website since before a lot of people knew what that website was, and for a while I used to cover a fair amount of news.[1] That necessitated knowing what was going on at all times, which necessitated being on Twitter, which up until that point had just been an app on my phone that I only remembered when I wanted to make fun of my college's student government meetings to an audience of 120 followers. I used Facebook because I was a human

---

[1] Early on I interviewed a woman for a story I was writing, and at the end she asked if I worked for a shoe website. "Excuse me?" I said. "You know," she replied, "*Buzz–Feet.*"

and Instagram mostly so I could post pictures of my crafts and badly lit meals, but getting into Twitter ratcheted my Internet engagement up by roughly 800 percent.

I loved it, at first. I loved how fast and funny everyone was, and that occasionally I could be fast and funny right back. I liked the instant gratification of getting favs and retweets, and meeting new people who occasionally became real-life friends, and the sense that there was always this current of commentary and action and reaction bubbling underneath the surface of whatever was happening out in the world. I felt like I was in on something, like finally my sense of humor and my obsessiveness had a place to land. I had a second computer monitor on my desk at work and I would keep Twitter open on it all day, burbling and flashing in the corner of my eye.

Does that sound kind of like a nightmare? Because, yeah, you're not wrong. I don't know if Twitter changed or if I did but after a year or two of having my feed constantly scrolling next to whatever I was doing at work or at home or on my phone, I started to get fatigued.

First, it was because there were a few people whose updates I did not want to see anymore: boys I'd dated who it hadn't worked out with, other journalists who made mean and totally unconstructive comments about their peers, anyone who seemed to use it only to perform their unilateral success/cynicism/posture that there's no way a person could assume literally all of the time. I acquainted myself with the Mute button and went along, figuring we can choose who we follow and that plenty of people probably found me irritating as heck too. (After all, pretty much all I tweeted about was yarn, ice-cream trucks, and my newly acquired pet snail.)

But then the problem started to feel systemic. The cycles started to get shorter, more frantic, and more staccato: a thing happened, people reacted, people reacted to the reactions, people mocked the reactions and the reactions to the reactions, new information emerged and got folded into the reactions and the reactions to the reactions and the mocking thereof, a new thing happened, people tried to compare and combine the two happenings and oh my God it gets so, so incredibly exhausting.

I watched countless cycles (which is too neat a word for the ragged rush of it all) and participated in many myself, all while I probably would have been better served doing something else. (For example: my job.) And the answer should be obvious: Just . . . don't! Look away!

Whenever I tried to explain it to my non-Internetty friends or my therapist, I could barely articulate why that didn't feel like an option. The closest analogy I can come up with is that Twitter, at least my corner of it, is sort of like a high school cafeteria. You've got your friends and your frenemies, and the people you want to be friends with and the ones you want to make out with and the older kids who don't know you exist so you just sit quietly and listen. You don't just opt out of the cafeteria, especially once you've already started eating there. You'd worry too much about missing something, or, worse, that people would talk about you if you're not around.

But of course you won't miss anything, because whatever it is will be distilled throughout the water supply in a matter of hours anyway. And doubly, of course, nobody cares about you nearly as much as you do. This is a good thing! But it's almost impossible to remember when you've been living in such a heightened environment, where every little message you compose is an opportunity for a miniature success or an itty-bitty failure. Because the feelings the Internet evokes are real; the things that happen there are real. Checking my phone a hundred times an hour has become less about strengthening connections and much more about satisfying compulsions; less about seeking pleasure and more about avoiding . . . what? Pain? Boredom? The unending march of my own mortality? I can't explain it, which is probably why I keep coming back for more.

So it should come as no surprise that my favorite social network isn't Twitter. It's not Facebook (too many engagement rings and former high school classmates arguing about making America great again), nor is it Instagram (I can look at the sunset too). It's a site called Ravelry. It has about 5 million users, and it's where knitters and crocheters and yarny types of all sorts find their people. It comprises a massive database where you can look up patterns for free or for sale by the designers, and find projects other users have made, and even figure out what to do with a particular skein of yarn. You can join groups and forums (my favorite is dedicated to finding patterns that look like wildly overpriced Anthropologie items) and you can post pictures of your own work.

"Are you on Ravelry?" is one of the first questions a fiber enthusiast asks another when they meet for the first time. Or best of all: "Oh yeah, I think I know you from Ravelry!"

That first summer I really committed to knitting, my first stop was a website called Knitty. It's an online magazine run by a woman named Amy Singer, and every season they post a new batch of weird, wonderful, and, most important, free patterns from a wide variety of designers. It was one of the first results whenever I blindly Googled things like "cute free knitting pattern sweater easy???" I remember the names of some of those designers as if they were celebrities: Beautia Dew, Jane Richmond, Lee Meredith. And I remember how each pattern is organized on a scale from "mellow" (easy) through "tangy," "piquant," and "extraspicy." I turned those names and those words over and over again in my head like rocks through a tumbler, the same way I'd once done with "afghan."

The thing about Knitty is that it was (and is) *good*. It was funny and down-to-earth and featured items I'd actually want to be seen wearing in public. There was no end to free online knitting patterns even when I was first poking around, in the late 1990s and early 2000s, but most of them seemed to be hosted on Geocities-looking blogs that could barely support the weight of the images. There were books, of course, but when the urge to make an off-the-shoulder pullover would strike me in the middle of one of those sleepless summer nights, I wanted ideas served up in front of me right away. I wanted millions of ideas! I wanted them organized and searchable, I wanted comments and corrections, I wanted them to pulse and shape-shift and inhabit the same world that I did.

Enter Ravelry. I'd noticed references to it sprinkled throughout Knitty and finally created an account (probably at three in the morning). It was everything I'd never thought to want, this portal to every conceivable type of pattern. I spent hours just scrolling through images, marveling at what thousands of people had created and dreaming up ways to make my own stuff. I started Frankensteining, combining the sleeves from one sweater, say, with the shaping and pocket details of another (in a yarn suggested for use in something else altogether). I'd always had this prejudice that patterns were restrictive, that all you were doing was copying someone else's work; stumbling upon this trove, however, showed me that they could be starting points, some scaffolding to build my own projects around. It also helped that I finally learned how to read them.

And beyond the technical stuff, Ravelry showed me that even surrounded by nobody but my yarn collection in my childhood bedroom, I wasn't alone. When I'd hit a tricky part on a project, I'd consult the comments. Most of the time, someone else had been there too, and had a suggestion for how to change your tension or bind off a couple of stitches in order to correct it. Or if they didn't have advice, they were only too happy to commiserate. I liked to lurk in forums and read the stories people posted about knitting for their children and grandchildren, for their congregations and charities and local biker gangs. I've always been a tad too lazy to regularly post my own projects, but I'm only too happy to wade through everyone else's.

Ravelry made me realize there was an entire Internet just for crafters. Through these channels I found *Cast On*, my first favorite podcast, run by a knitter named Brenda Dayne, who has probably the most melodic voice ever to broadcast on the airwaves. I delayed looking up her picture for almost a year because I liked to imagine her as this little musical bubble, drifting over the Welsh countryside in between piles of newly spun yarn. Once I'd exhausted the *Cast On* archives (RIP), I looked for other podcasts, fiber-related and not; I discovered that I crafted best surrounded by sound, not glancing up and down at the TV or in silence. I'd always sort of thought crafting was supposed to be quiet, save for the click of your needles or the murmured conversation of your sewing circle for gnarled spinsters or whatever, and realized it didn't have to be—that, in fact, it could be accompanied by the sound of other people *talking about crafting*. This opened up a floodgate of information and stories and even a few half-assed attempts to make a show of my own. I consumed a whole lot, and it made me want to start putting something out in return.

The Internet was what notified me about an event called the New York State Sheep and Wool Festival, which takes place in Rhinebeck, half an hour from where I went to college, and another called Vogue Knitting Live!, which takes place thirty blocks from my former office in Manhattan. I've gone to Rhinebeck for the past eight years and Vogue Knitting for the past four, and they're the highlight of their respective seasons. The former takes place in a Hudson Valley fairground, replete with hot apple cider and herding dogs, and the latter is in the towering Marriott Marquis in Times Square, but they're both designed to bring crafters together. (I've heard them each referred to as a "knitter prom.") They feature classes taught by experts in everything from weaving to wool dyeing to how to make swants.[2] There are dozens of booths with yarn, tools, and homemade knickknacks for sale. And everywhere, people meeting for the first time, hugging like old friends and checking out one another's name tags. "Oh, right, I know you from Ravelry!"

Also, yarn. Did I mention you can buy yarn? With money? All of your money? That's really what I'm after when I attend these events; sure, it's great to check out what new techniques people are using, and to say hello to friends who I only get to see once or twice a year, and to feel like I'm finally among folks who appreciate what I've done with a single ball of Malabrigo, who admire the disappearing cable on the yoke of my sweater, who understand this small but constant part of who I am.

But real talk, it's all about the yarn. I don't know a crafter alive who can resist the allure of booth after booth piled high with warm, squishy goodness. All those colors! All that poten-

---

[2] Sweater-pants, which is when you turn a wacky old sweater into a pair of pants. It's the brainchild of a knitwear designer named Steven West and everyone should own some.

tial! Sometimes I set a budget before I go to Rhinebeck or Vogue Knitting, but I always manage to give myself a loophole the instant I spot an especially alluring splurge.

Just don't buy lunch this week! I'll tell myself. *That's easily $50 extra right there, which is basically the same as $150, which if you round up is $200!*[3] *God, you're so fiscally responsible.*

Another thing the Internet does is make it easy to drop dollars on yarn even when you are not at a convention or in a yarn store. I don't shop online too often because my MO is more "orbit the shop or booth for forty minutes while intermittently rubbing the yarn in question against various parts of my body," but every now and then a digital yarn spree hits the spot. I've gotten a few duds this way—a rainbow best described in person as "clown barf," a supposed "soft green" that turned out to be so neon it was difficult to look at directly—but the same has been true for yarn I've bought in a store, even after all that deliberation. It's just like buying clothes, or picking someone up at a bar: sometimes you get home, dump it on your bed, and are like, *Ehh, the lighting in there must have been bad.*

And as the old adage goes, where the Internet taketh away (my money), it also giveth (me a little bit of money, sometimes).

---

[3] Non-crafters are always *floored* by how much yarn can cost. There's a range, as with most things in this delightful late-capitalist society, but if I'm going to make a sweater I know that I'll most likely spend at bare minimum $60. And some of my favorite yarns will run me twice that. There are times when I feel guilty about spending so much, but then I remind myself that I've always been too nervous a person to really enjoy smoking weed, etc., so I save a lot of money that I might otherwise spend on, like, drugs. Yarn is drugs.

I rarely knit for money, unless it's a commission by a very close friend, because the materials are so expensive and the process is so time-consuming that if I wanted anything close to a fair rate I'd have to charge around $300 for a sweater. And I am not good enough to make a $300 sweater/the pressure overall seems very stressful/I like my friends too much to charge them like that and so if I want someone to have a handmade sweater I just give them the goddamn sweater.

But! These problems do not extend to embroidery. Embroidery takes relatively little time and only a few dollars' worth of materials, and thus has become my twee side hustle. About two years ago a former coworker posted on Facebook, looking for someone to make a custom embroidery for his roommate. I'd never done a commission before but had been doing samplers for long enough that I figured I'd give it a shot. Besides, I was in a period where I felt totally sick of waiting for someone to tell me I was good enough to pursue something that sounded interesting; I'd spent a large chunk of my school and then work life figuring that there were people who were better qualified than I was for projects or promotions or leadership roles, but I was always happiest when I put the horse before the cart and just went for it anyway. Dudes seemed to do this all the time to great effect. I don't advocate faking it until you make it on, like, the operating table, but when it comes to stitching an inside joke and a doodle on a six-inch piece of fabric, lean the ever-loving heck in.

When I'd given my friend the piece (and confirmed that it had already been gifted to its rightful owner) I posted a picture of it on my various social media feeds. And requests came . . . not pouring in, but trickling in, like a garden hose left unattended. Most orders came from coworkers and friends: a *Lord of the Rings* quote for a boyfriend, a song lyric for a mother, an embroidered array of gluten-full goodies for a hapless Celiac. I did a rush order for a colleague who had forgotten his anniversary; I did a fairly lifelike portrait of the Food Network chef Bobby Flay. I've done a few for people I've never met, mostly friends of friends or people from Twitter, and shipped them to Nebraska and California and Chicago.

Some people know exactly what they want—a color scheme, a specific image—but most only care about the words and leave me to make up the rest. I worried at first that doing commissions would feel rote, even a little stifling, but it's turned out to be just the right amount of restriction to make me get creative. I didn't know I could stitch a tiny, perfect doughnut or Bobby Flay's face until someone asked me to. How do I illustrate this quote I've never heard before? How do I write out names and words that mean so much to someone else?

That's the best part of doing custom embroideries: getting access to that kind of intimacy. Being the conduit, however invisibly, for someone I care about to say something of value to someone they care about. Nobody's ordering expensive, time-consuming craft projects to tell their enemies to fuck right off;

these are all expressions of deep love, even if they're silly. One of my earliest pieces was for a coworker whose friend had said something ridiculous yet quasi-brilliant while drunk: "Why is it you only ever run into people you already know?"

My coworker hired me to commemorate this almost-koan forever (or at least as long as the fabric and thread last). But even something so jokey and seemingly throwaway takes on a certain weight when it's been written down on something more permanent than paper or a screen: *I hear you. I see you. The things you say and do matter to me, and will be remembered.*

If the order is a lyric, I like to listen to the song while I work; if it's a quote, I'll find the clip or the paragraph, put it in its original context even though my job is to make a new one. I've absolutely teared up while making them: "I fucking love you." "You're my person." And I've gotten ideas for my own pieces, for myself and for the people in my life. "The best is yet to come," I stitched for Aude after a birthday and a breakup, surrounded by a bunch of small stars I'd learned to make for a recent commission. I document them all on Instagram, and sometimes even Twitter, and ask that my customers send me photos of the pieces in their new homes. I like to have a record of all these little records.

And then there are the people you meet. Not long ago, I met a girl I knew from the Internet. She'd tweeted at me, we'd emailed back and forth, moved it to Facebook, and then finally arranged to have coffee. She'd read some of my writing about crafting and anxiety and that's why she'd initially reached out; she was starting a company, she told me, that used knitting as a jumping-off point to talk about mental health. Obviously I was all in.

You get a lot of the same comments when you write online: "Somebody got paid to write this?" "Go home [your name or the name of the publication], you're drunk." "Ain't nobody got time for that!" (This last especially when you suggest that perhaps readers might enjoy taking the time to make something with their hands.) You learn to ignore them, to occasionally gain insight from them, and mostly to consider them an annoying but necessary part of the ecosystem in which you choose to reside.

But every so often you get a message like this: "Thank you for putting this into words. I thought I was alone." These weigh so much more than the tossed-off, dismissive comments that even just one every couple of weeks or months can be enough to sustain you.

And even more rarely, one of those messages turns into an actual connection. When Danielle arrived at my office for our coffee date, she had a gift. It was a pink-and-purple cowl that she'd knitted in a loose, ropelike pattern. I kept it on the table beside me, patting it throughout our excellent and far-ranging conversation. It had been so long since someone had knitted for me. This makes sense—coals to Newcastle, right?—but I think maybe other crafters are the people we should most want to craft for. I appreciated every stitch of that cowl, every minute I knew she had spent turning the yarn into a gift for someone she only knew through a screen. I wasn't—I never have been—alone.

Tools of the Trade

~~~~~~

When someone expresses the desire to learn a craft, whether it's knitting, crochet, or whatever else, the thing that always seems to scare them the most is the prospect of picking out supplies.

"So you need, like . . . needles?" they ask. I tell them yes, or a hook, and they look relieved—they knew, at least, that much. The rest should be a piece of cake. And then I have to bring up the concept of needle size (thin for lace and socks, medium for sweaters, thick for cowls and hats, but none of that is really a hard and fast rule) and materials (wood, aluminum, plastic), not to mention varieties (straight, circular, double-pointed), and the person is once again stricken, even more lost than before. I have to explain that it'll be fine, it's just like picking out the right ingredients at the supermarket; yeah, cucumbers and zucchini might look the same to the untrained eye, but once you know the difference you'll be cooking in no time. Sometimes the prospective student listens and is mollified by this, but mostly they stay simmering at a low-grade panic until I agree to accompany them to the store.

I get it; crafting is supposed to be this simple, meditative activity, and then all of a sudden there are all these *factors* involved. If someone were to tell me to pinch-hit on their baseball team or babysit their child, I would have similar difficulty figuring out what to pack in my bag—a glove, right, or some diapers? But how big is the glove supposed to be, and at what age are kids through with diapers, and then what do they do after that? Honestly, the sheer amount of *stuff* required to complete even the simplest task can be staggering, to the point where it's a miracle any of us ever try anything new at all.

Luckily, there are really only a few categories necessary to maintain a fairly steady crafting habit. Let's start with a bag, because that's recognizable to civilians. Most crafters have a bag to carry around their works in progress (WIPs) and to organize their other supplies. Some have many—a pouch for each individual WIP—but those people are much more organized than I am and also probably file their tax returns on January 2. Most, I would imagine, operate more haphazardly: a tote filled with other totes they call upon as needed, or a perplexing array of plastic grocery bags pierced with three different sizes of needles.

That is my craft-bag method—I grab one when I'm running out the door and can't stuff another in my already-overflowing backpack, or when a project is especially delicate and shouldn't have to share living space with the rest of the things I lug around (usually a makeup case, my glasses, my sunglasses, my Game Boy, a book, a phone charger, assorted jewelry I threw on before leaving the house one day and then decided was too much and never had the wherewithal to remove from the inner pocket and so it's all tangled in an inextricable brass blob, and half a Xanax I mostly just like knowing is there). When I was young I was known for my bag, as much as you can be known for anything in the halls of an elementary school. It was a black canvas tote, screen-printed with the multicolored logo of the San Francisco Museum of Modern Art, where I had not and still have never been but where one of my closest friends now works. (The world is funny that way.) My sister, Moriah, used to have a matching hat until she left it on a plane, ending her tenure as an outrageously adorable little acorn head who looked like she'd wandered off the set of an art-school remake of *The Sandlot*.

It wasn't the appearance of the bag that made my classmates smirk and my teachers smile benevolently, but the contents. Inside it I kept a variety of books, as many as six or seven at a time, so that whenever I finished the one I was reading I'd have plenty of options for the next. How could I know what I'd want to read in an hour, two hours, a whole entire school day? What if the ending of the book I was currently inhaling had a surprise twist that made me crave normalcy; what if the bus ride home jogged a desire for a mystery rather than a fantasy? Even at age eight I hated the thought of being bound, of not having control over my (however immediate, however minuscule) future.

Occasionally I would make room in my bag for my knitting. I liked to knit during circle time and whenever my teachers read aloud. I wasn't supposed to be doing anything else with my hands, I reasoned, so why not let them do what they wanted while my mind relaxed? Some, like my marvelous fifth-grade teacher, went along with it, but not all of them; in third grade, an aide called me out in front of the entire class, telling me to put that away, I was supposed to be paying attention. My cheeks burned and I thought about running from the room, but I stayed where I was and stuffed the yarn deep into my bag.

I did not know, as a child deathly afraid of getting in trouble, how to say that working on that half-done scarf helped me pay *better* attention. The stitches kept me from fidgeting, from biting my nails and twirling my hair and staring at the clock. They kept me from doodling in my notebooks and in the margins of library books. They certainly kept me from grabbing one of the slimmer paperbacks I carted around and tucking it into my textbook, which I liked to do whenever I finished skimming whatever section I was supposed to be concentrating on. My bag contained half a dozen tiny promises that I would never be bored, that I would always be understood, even if the drudgery and the teasing at school got to be too much.

Nobody makes fun of my glasses anymore (to my face), and

my bag now contains more than just novels, but it serves the same purpose. It's a safeguard. It means that no matter how long the subway is stuck belowground, no matter how tedious or tense the work meeting, I can still find a way to channel my energy. I wonder about the people who don't have a bag. Mostly they seem to be men: they get on and off the train with their hands shoved in their pockets, earbuds nestled in their skulls, nothing to weigh them down beyond the miniature supercomputers they cradle like baby doves (which, invariably, do not have phone cases). I don't know if I envy or pity people like this, unladen but also unready. Unconcerned, maybe. Unburdened. The rare times I walk around with no bag—coming back from the Laundromat, maybe, or a run that turned into a stroll—I've felt suspiciously light. But it's a lightness that comes with its own weight, its own worries, as pleasant and yet as slimy as when I had my braces removed and slid my tongue over my untethered teeth for the first time.

Once you have your bag, you have to get your scissors. Not so hard, right? Every kitchen and office supply closet has these. But there's a mundane yet dangerous allure to scissors, especially when you are little. This makes sense: they are most likely introduced to you as belonging entirely to the realm of adults. Even if you are a good kid, scissors beckon. (See: me at age five, cutting my then baby sister's hair and hiding it in our toy box.)

They live in cups on the teacher's desk and in your parents' miscellaneous-stuff drawer and in the hands of hairstylists. They're like knives, but less scary; swords, but more real. At first you're allowed to use them only in specific, supervised situations, and you must never, ever run with them. They have the power to make things less, and so they can impart it, briefly, to you.

Now I am an adult, for all intents and purposes, and own at least five or six pairs of scissors, scattered throughout my apartment. When it comes to crafting, they mostly come into play at crucial junctures: in the very beginning, as you cut your fabric or remove the bindings from your new yarn; at turning points, when you switch a color or complete a section; and at the end, when they really prove their worth. Scissors are for neatening up, for putting in order, for that final sprucing skim before a piece is finally complete. There's nothing more unsatisfying than finishing a long knitting or crochet project when you're out for the day and don't have a pair of scissors on hand to tidy up the loose yarn ends; it just looks diminished and undignified, like someone who's come home from a long journey and hasn't yet had time to shower.

If you have to use scissors at some other point, it's usually a matter of triage: fixing a snarl, working around a snag, rescuing a piece that's been crumpled in the depths of a bag it should never have been shoved into. For some reason, this happens to me most frequently with socks. Maybe because they're small enough that I take them with me everywhere, or maybe because they're knitted on double-pointed needles, so there are many times more tips from which stitches can slip off. Regardless, I've watched in mute horror as I plunge my hand into my bag and remove what looks like a dust bunny made animate, jaws clamped around the memory of my clearly-not-that-beloved project.

In those moments, scissors are my kindest, firmest friend. They watch as I try in vain to rewind the ball of yarn, to follow what could logically only be one strand but feels more like five back to the point where it connects with the knitting. They say nothing as I tug, sit silently as I swear, and finally, when I say uncle, step in and with one motion sever the problem from my life. I salvage what yarn I can and rewind it in a calmer if diminished version of itself. I reattach it to the project and vow to weave in the loose ends later. I keep going.

Where new crafters start to get tripped up is somewhere around the word "needle." "Needle" can refer to a huge range of objects, each more daunting than the last.

There are sewing and embroidery needles, small and sharp and always disappearing right when you need them and re-appearing in the sole of your bare foot hours later. These can be used to make pictures and words, to close up the edges of brand-new objects, but they can also be called upon for on-the-spot repairs: tears, escapee buttons, ragged hems. Keeping a needle and thread nearby is a small price to pay for the kind of help you can lend someone (or yourself) in these quietly dire moments. There are tapestry needles, otherwise known as yarn needles, meant to weave in the loose ends caused by scissors and endings. There are felting needles, terrifyingly jagged, with a broad handle that you clutch as you stab and agitate wool. Cable needles have a dip in the middle to patiently hold your stitches while you work on others out of order. Sewing machines have needles affixed to their front arms and are an unholy bitch to thread, and crochet hooks aren't needles at all but it's totally understandable to refer to them as such.

All of them simple, all of them serving their different purposes, but all meant to do, largely, the same thing: plunge into the nebulous softness of your materials and tame them. They're the bridge between what you have and what you want. Even though your route might be twisty and turny, full of mistakes and backtracks, needles are comforting in their persistent linearity, their definite end points, even their interchangeability. (You might have your preferences, but any tapestry needle will do when push comes to shove.) Yarn and fabric are slippery, each with an energy all its own. They represent possibility but also uncertainty, a certain impenetrability that taunts you until you're reasonably sure you know what you want them to be. Needles don't do that. They lack life until you pick them up and return it to them. And once you master them, they become an extension of you.

Finally, there are knitting needles. I must own at least fifty sets—in bamboo and aluminum, circular and straight, short little double-points and long, unwieldy single-points. One of my first big purchases when I got my first job was a set of needles with an array of removable tips. It felt like I had bought the world; suddenly I didn't need to hunt down a pair of size 8s right when I needed them, nor buy a new set of 10s or 15s when a pattern called for them halfway through. I could simply twist off the tips and replace them with different sizes, all laid out before me in a neat black binder. I liked being the kind of person with the foresight and the means to possess all the tools she could ever need. I liked that I had a system.

But in a slow fit of entropy, the system broke down. A 6 would find its way into the slot meant for a 7; a 4 was bent so far out of shape that it more closely resembled a cable needle. I started leaving the tips in various jars and bags around my room, and then came the day when I desperately needed a set of 9s and couldn't find them, and so finally I just went out and bought new ones. I was frustrated with myself—that was money I'd already spent, an investment I'd made—but then I got over it. The system had been meant to help me, not to make me feel guilty when I couldn't perfectly adhere to it. I bought more needles, and then another set of interchangeables, and gave some away to students, and sometimes I can find exactly what I need when I need it and sometimes I can't. I am doing my best.

When my grandma died, I didn't take much from her house. Partly because my apartment is small, unable to handle much beyond the essentials I've already collected. There isn't room for an inlaid end table or a spare armchair. But even her books and knickknacks didn't call out to me. They felt like such a product of the space they occupied that taking them out of it seemed like it might sap them of all magic, all memories. I accepted just a couple of knitting booklets my mother dug up as she packed up the house to sell it, and a single-serving French press.

I didn't even want any of her considerable yarn collection. They weren't really my preferred colors (she favored dusty pastels while I go either full-on Day-Glo or neutral as heck), but that wasn't fully the reason; I'd loved to plunder it while she was still alive. It had felt, in some small way, like a collaboration: her materials, my execution. I usually used her yarn to make little things, tiny bowls or ornament-sized sweaters. I liked showing my grandma what I'd coaxed forth from her yarn, so different from the afghans she made from the very same material, the large beside the small. Without her, there wasn't anyone to show.

The only things I found myself truly wanting after she died were her knitting needles. In the den next to the bedroom where Moriah and I had always slept on visits was a corner devoted to my grandma's crafting: a closet lined with plastic organizers full of yarn, her sewing machine, her ironing board, and a large chest of drawers that contained all of her other tools. These, and the yarn, were always arranged perfectly in order, as if they floated back to their assigned spaces once she was done with them.

In their own drawer lived a neat display of knitting needles and crochet hooks. My grandma didn't have nearly as many as I do, because she didn't need to: all of hers were clearly visible, organized by type and size. Whenever she needed a particular set, there it was. I'd pilfered those, too, on my visits; whenever I'd return from the fancy yarn store in town with a new haul, I'd run to her drawers. Sometimes I returned them before I left and sometimes I didn't. My grandma never minded. In the last years of her life, she encouraged me to take whatever I wanted. She didn't knit anymore.

After her funeral, when we returned to her empty-but-still-full house, I went right to the craft corner. I didn't even take off my shoes or jacket; I didn't know where else to go. I picked up almost every single needle, turned them over in my hands, prodded the tips with my fingers. I didn't take all of them, just the ones that filled the holes in my collection, and the ones that reminded me the most of her.

Months later, I'd loan a pair to a friend just learning for the first time. She's a cook and took to the repetitive motions instantly, loved the gray cowl she cast on with me so much that she took the project home with her for the holidays. When she came back, she apologized up and down: her baby cousin had broken one of the needles. I didn't care, and I didn't think my grandma would either. They'd already served their purpose, venturing out into the world and allowing someone new to fall in love with knitting. Besides, I had others.

And the Girlfriend Sweater, the gray cabled one I made for myself instead of any boy, that came to be on my grandma's needles too. I would have gotten the same results with any twenty-four-inch size 5 circulars, but I loved looking down at the light-gray aluminum darting in and out of the yarn and imagining them in my grandma's hands. Hands that played piano, that planted gardens, that rubbed my back and my sister's and my mother's and her sister's. Hands whose leathery firmness I won't ever feel again, that will never again rub my back, that will never hold my children. But they did the work they set out to do.

Her needles made my finished sweater feel like it was imbued with a promise, that I came from somewhere, that I had been and would be so, so loved. And when I cast off, the needles slipped into my messy collection and blended in right away. I'm not even sure today which ones they are! But I don't feel too precious about them. I just like knowing that they're there.

Small, Surprising Things That Remind Me of the Feeling of Crafting

1. When the bartender gives you a free drink, or at least remembers your usual order.
2. When you crave a food and then acquire the food in a timely manner and it's exactly like you imagined.
3. Arriving at home and realizing you are alone and that it's clean.
4. Laundry that's still warm from the dryer.
5. Good, comfortable sex.
6. When you are tasked with opening the bottle of wine and you do so on the first try.
7. When a new acquaintance you like a lot invites you to something out of the blue.
8. When a cool stranger compliments your eyeliner or jacket.
9. Eavesdropping on a really juicy conversation.

10. Finishing the crossword, with or without help.
11. Buying a new outfit and wearing it that same day.
12. Singing in a choir.
13. Underlining a particularly moving passage in a book with a particularly smooth pen.

Homemaking

~~~~~~

After her father and then her mother died, my mom went back to the house in Virginia where she grew up. She'd been back and forth plenty over the previous year, she and her sister, Kathleen, checking in on their now-widowed mother, taking care of the place, and eventually moving her into an assisted-living facility. My grandma stayed there only a few days before, a touch defiantly, she died.

And so it fell to my mom to do one of the things she is best at: make a home. She had helped us kids set up our dorm rooms and apartments, had presided over the renovation of our house in Boston and the purchase of a small beachside place in Rhode Island. She'd even tried to work her magic on her mother's room at the facility, not knowing it would be inhabited for such a short time; she returned the armchair that had sat, almost unused, in the corner. My mother knows how to look at the smallest, bleakest space and transpose everything you'd need to make it cozy, to make it feel like you. She helps us pick out all our furniture and hangs our shelves and paints our walls, no matter how fussy the terms of the lease.

This time, though, would be in reverse. My mom, Kathleen, and their brother, Michael, had decided to sell the house, and so it needed to be cleaned out and staged for future inhabitants. My mom kept texting us pictures that looked like they belonged on HGTV: the basement den where my grandma had kept her craft supplies, now transformed into a modern seating area; the soft, squishy living room where we'd crowded on top of one another to open Christmas presents all of a sudden rendered in clean, straight lines, with a coffee table in the middle that totally would have gotten in Santa's way.

The house looked smaller in those photographs than I remembered, probably because in the twenty-five years I spent visiting, I never really thought of it as a house. It was more like a country, ruled over by the twin guardians who were my grandparents: Grandpa, tall and peaceful, and Grandma, small and fierce and loving.

But of course it was a house, and it had already been a home, for a long, long time. It was where my mom and Kathleen and Michael had grown up (apart from stints in New Jersey and England) and where Matthew, Moriah, and I spent vacations. We would enter the house and it would swallow us, with its familiar smells (pine needles and cats, but in a good way) and its mythical supply of knickknacks (a vase full of peacock feathers, a carved wooden elephant on every surface, always a Whitman's Sampler somewhere to be excavated for its caramels and maple creams). Even when we reached our twenties, Moriah and I would run down to the basement bedroom we shared— I used to "suggest" that she sleep on a cot next to the bed, but in later years we each just picked a side—and one of us would immediately jump on the ancient gold exercise bike parked in front of the TV. We'd take turns slowly pedaling while watching a steady stream of *Degrassi* episodes and Christmas-movie marathons, each promising the other we wouldn't peek as she wrapped her pile of gifts.

Our bedroom was full of relics. In the far corner stood cabinets piled high with my grandpa's patents and research papers. He had taught mechanical engineering at Virginia Tech, an enormous university down the street that seems to take up half the town. It's where my mom and her siblings went to school, and where my grandma worked in the sociology department for years. (It's also where, in 2007, thirty-two students were killed by their classmate, who went on to shoot himself. There is now a massive memorial that kids who weren't even born back then run around. If someone's heard of Blacksburg before, this is often why.)

Across from the bed was a floor-to-ceiling set of shelves displaying photos of my grandma as a young model, as a student, as a sister and wife and mother, and, always, as a grandmother. There she was, holding Moriah, fresh from the bath with her adorable cap of hair. There was baby me, alone and practically bald, examining what looked like a seashell on the beach but upon closer inspection was probably a cigarette butt. (My mom and I couldn't stop laughing when we figured that out.) We all looked so happy.

We'd often be woken up in the morning by Grandma or Kathleen coming into the room so they could let out the resident cat.[1] There was always a rotating cast of cats; my grandparents fed the neighborhood strays, eventually constructing what we called the "cat condo"—a sprawling outdoor structure with different heated compartments and a roof to protect their furry visitors from the Virginia elements. Eventually a cat would attach itself to the family and move into the main house. When one died, before too long another would come and take its spot, although each cat held a special place in the family's collective memory: Franklin, Spooky, Purdy, Bosco, Goldilocks, Harry.

My mom and Kathleen packed away the photos. They donated the exercise bike to a local thrift store and the cat condo to a nearby farm. They made the house ready to become someone else's home, now that their folks were both gone.

My mom and I have always been extremely close. For a while, it was just the two of us and my dad—they like to tell me of when they first brought me home from the hospital, put me on the

---

[1] In their defense, "morning" is kind of a strong word—my grandparents' house had that particular back-home magic that causes you to sleep until noon long after you've aged out of that sluggish habit.

dining-room table, and realized they had absolutely no idea what to do next. But they figured it out, and soon enough there was Moriah, three-and-change years after me, and then Matthew, three-and-change years after her. Before them, though, before I could walk or read or recognize my reflection in a mirror, my mom and I started talking. We still do talk constantly, about our feelings and feelings *about* those feelings, about books and movies and music, about how we spent our days and what we're looking forward to next. We'd talk as she drove me to and from school and choir practice, and then as she drove me to and from college. Now we talk on the phone most days, in little snippets as I'm walking to the subway or she's walking the dog, between her visits to New York and mine to Boston and Rhode Island. Also, she's gotten really good at texting.

She is, in a word, dope. Lots of people think their mother is the best, but I have to make a strong argument in favor of mine. There's the matter of her name, for starters: Pamela Joy Furey. Joy! Furey! It's so perfect that if this were fiction it would sound too on-the-nose and I would have to cut it. I like my name a lot, but I've always resented the fact that if my parents had cared more about my don't-fuck-with-me quotient, they would have at least thought to name me Alanna Okun-Furey. There's also the fact that my mother is a drummer. She's played since high school—I used to try on the white majorette boots that were relegated to our Halloween costume bin and stomp around—but really doubled down once we kids grew up, taking lessons in town and sharing a drum kit with Matthew. (They are around the same height.) She plays in klezmer bands and in pit orchestras for musicals.[2] Once, Matthew was slated to play drums for a summer production of *The Music Man*, and realized at the last minute that he wouldn't be able to make one of the performances. He frantically texted our mom and she showed up without complaint, twice the age of anyone else involved in the show.

Growing up, I didn't fully appreciate the magnitude of my mom's ability to make a home. Our house was nice, but it also just *was*. She inherited my grandma's penchant for vases of feathers and bowls of orbs; the living room in particular is full of tchotchkes that, if you stare long enough, are truly bonkers: a large brass pear with a keyhole in the middle, a ladder that leads . . . nowhere. She prefers understated palettes (you can't possibly know how many shades of taupe there are in the universe until you've spent forty-five minutes with my mom at Benjamin Moore) and is a genius at getting furniture retailers to sell her floor models at a deep discount. But there's nothing fussy about her taste; one of her great joys is when we're all clustered around the granite island in the kitchen, or draped over one another on the giant couch in the sunroom. Her even greater joy is when we all go to sleep and she can have those rooms to

---

2 Klezmer is like jazzy Jewish folk music, and her primary band is called—honest to God—Too Klez for Comfort.

herself and her design magazines. For a while, she worked for an architect, and then went on to consult on home renovations, doing for other people what she'd already done for us.

And she was there to oversee the design of each one of my homes, no matter how short a time I'd be there. She'd help me figure out what I needed to buy (and usually wind up paying for it), sketch out floor plans on napkins and in newspaper margins, and drive me and all my earthly possessions up and down the East Coast. She would construct IKEA furniture, drill holes in walls that were essentially cardboard-covered concrete, and disguise hideous light fixtures or school-issued furniture that we weren't allowed to just get rid of.

"Whoa," a friend said upon walking into my room junior year of college, the first time I had my very own single. "This is, like, a *home*."

It was. My mother had stayed for two days, sleeping on an air mattress she'd brought from Boston. The room had been a disaster, all the furniture pushed aside in order to make space. I'd gotten annoyed with her; there wasn't enough room for both of us to work, so I stood by and watched as she measured and marked and nailed her way through each task.

"It looks fine to me," I said, seven or eight times.

"I'll be done soon," she would reply breezily. I left and went down the hall to see my friends, and to whine that my mother was a maniac.

When the room was finished, she called me back in and I cried. The dusty red curtains we'd picked out together fluttered in the late-summer wind; the four light fixtures meant to replace the glaring overhead glowed softly; the two strange paintings of pears I'd found at IKEA hung side by side like they were displayed in a gallery. I cried because it was just mine, and because she had been the one to make it so. That my mother could come into this space with a few disparate things I'd kind of sort of liked a little and create a home so uncannily mine— that was what did it. My room was proof that I was loved.

She did it again when I got my first apartment in New York, and then again when I moved to my own place. (I still have the curtains and the pears.) She did it for Moriah in her dorm rooms and in her apartments off campus in St. Louis, and for Matthew just ten minutes away from our house in Boston. When we got the place in Rhode Island, my mother would spend her weekends out there, using the bathrooms at Town Hall and Walmart because the water wasn't yet turned on. She painted and rearranged and picked out a collection of furniture and tchotchkes that are just this side of nautical: no lobsters wearing sailor hats, but a whole bunch of knots. Each of these homes is like her—warm, open, practical with a few quirky touches—but they all feel different, reflective of those of us who live and grow there. Home always felt so natural, so effortless, that I didn't appreciate how much work went into making one until I started to build my own.

I spent a large part of my first year living alone pleading for my mother to come back to my apartment and help me install the new curtains she'd given me for Christmas. The ceiling was too high, I didn't own a level, I was afraid I'd screw it up—I whined and I bargained. She promised she'd come visit me in the spring for my birthday, but then Moriah moved back home and was having too hard a time to be left alone; then my grandma got sick. Then it was July and then August and the curtains were still folded underneath my bedside table.

I started asking her about it once a week, even though I could feel myself being bratty, missing the point: when are you coming, why did you say you would if you didn't mean it, don't you love me enough to bring your drill and yourself for just a day or two?

This was not a new dynamic for us. "You *promised*," I muttered (or yelled) throughout my childhood. "It's not *fair*." That was the flip side of my mother's enduring care—the smallest, ugliest part of me thought I had to stake a claim on it to make sure there would always be enough. I wanted to earmark a chunk of her time, keep a tally, know for certain that no matter how old I got or how capable of handling my own problems, I could always call her up and she'd be there in minutes. Because the truth is, of course, that while her capacity for love is infinite, her time and energy do have limits. When Moriah started struggling with school and her mental health, it was my mom who flew out to St. Louis month after month; when my grandma started to fade, my mom was by her side.

My mom has always kept all of her important promises, despite my whining to the contrary. When she couldn't come through (which usually consisted of nothing more than being late to pick me up from musical rehearsal when Moriah had tennis and Matthew had guitar lessons), it was because she had so many other people and creatures to care for. She spends so much of herself building us up—our spaces, our creativity—that I sometimes worry there's not enough left over for her own use. I want everything for my mother, but I also want everything from her. It only recently occurred to me, years later, that I can hang curtains myself.

And in the fall, just a month after her mother's funeral, my mom did come to visit. She drilled and hammered, cleaned each slat on the blinds, and installed insulating plastic over the windows before she hung the curtains at last. They bring the whole room together.

My mother's parents got old quickly. They'd always been sharp and vital—I'd race my grandma for custody of the crossword every morning but it would nearly always be done by the time I made it upstairs—but one day my grandpa went into the hospital and never really left. He died in September, the day after my grandma's birthday, and then one year minus ten days later she died too. They had been married for sixty-two years.

Maybe the thing my mom and I have most in common is our love for having a project, and it turns out that death leaves you with a lot of them. There was the funeral to plan and the will to execute, the house to clean and sell. Her greatest superpower turned inside-out, the satisfaction of completing a room forced to live next to the grief over losing what it had once contained. She called me less frequently during this period, but the tone was more urgent. She wondered if the objects she sifted through, the ones she packed or threw away or donated, still held the spark of her old life, or had that gone away along with her parents? She was the one who cried on the phone now, even though she still left plenty of space for me to bemoan boys or work problems or whatever bullshit I was hung up on, and I did not know what to say other than that I was there, I loved her more than I would ever be able to express, there would be new life to build even as the old one fell apart.

I miss my grandparents all the time. I miss their support and their opinions, their styles and their smells. I miss life with them in it. But I have to say, I miss them most of all for my mom. I miss when she got to be a daughter too. Now I find myself wanting to *be* everything for her, daughter and friend and mother, all the while knowing that I can't—that, really, I shouldn't. I can't make a space for her where she feels as known and as safe as the one she's made for me. All I can do is live in mine, and invite her in, and do the same for someone else someday.

Pieces

~~~~~~

My sister makes baskets. She does this by sewing pieces of rope in intricate coils, dismantling the arms of sewing machines and investing in a lifetime supply of zip ties to hold everything together—our family Amazon account looks like it belongs to a serial killer with a flair for color. Some of the baskets are small, meant to house succulents or stray hair ties; some are shaped like vases or bongs. Some are meant to be hung from the ceiling or from the branches of trees, and others—the ones she made in art school—are meant to be worn, like diving helmets that are at once both cozy and deeply upsetting.

Sometimes she sells these baskets, at open markets in Boston and Rhode Island. Other times she gives them as gifts; I have at least three in my apartment right now, with my eye on a set of trivet-looking pieces she's been working on lately. Mostly, though, when I picture Moriah's baskets, I picture her hunched over the family dining table or her sewing space in our parents' house, intently weaving all those bits and pieces together, starting at the center and spiraling outward in ever-larger circles. To me, those materials look like they belong in the aisles of a hardware store (where many of them, in fact, are from); to her, they're a way to make a life.

I've tried a lot of other crafts. Knitting is my first love, crochet and embroidery my shared second, but I've dabbled in plenty of others. There was my brief stint with felting, the same process by which wool sweaters shrink down to hard, small versions of themselves when you throw them in the dryer (except, this time, on purpose); mostly I just ended up drawing a lot of blood with the sharp hook required for agitating the wool. There was sewing, which I've felt guilty about not really "getting" for my entire crafting life, which is almost as long as my entire actual life. I can repair basic holes, and piece a few easy things together by hand, but what's always drawn me to the yarnier crafts is that sense of making something out of nothing; I sort of hate the prospect of beginning with an overwhelming amount of material that you're meant to whittle down into a manageable shape.

Still, I always half thought I'd come back to it. I guess I'd hoped my grandma could reteach me, beyond the American Girl Doll pants she'd walked me through two decades previously.

When she died and I flew back to Virginia for the funeral,

one of the first things I did was pick a fight with Moriah over our grandma's sewing machine. Moriah had been there since the day before, helping our mom and Kathleen plan the funeral and start to pack up the house, and had already called dibs.

"That's the machine she taught me on," I hissed over lunch, suddenly filled with a possessiveness and anger that were desperate to manifest themselves this way. I hated the thought of Moriah taking it and modifying it for her own use, even though the odds of me actually ever using it were slim to none. I guess I wanted proof that I had mattered, that this was a special bond my grandma and I had shared, that everyone would just automatically know to give me this one thing.

"I just wanted something to remember her by," Moriah whispered back. She was trying not to cry. She spent a lot of time trying not to cry, which usually caused her to cry even more.

I felt trapped. I put my drink down too hard on the table, and the rest of the family looked up. I swallowed my misplaced rage and told her we'd talk about it later. It's not that I felt like I was the Crafter except maybe, in this grasping little part of me, I did.

Which brings us, indirectly, to weaving. In a fit of I don't know what, a few years ago I bought a small loom that was intended for children, and spent a couple of months making wall hangings. I loved it—it's the perfect way to use up leftover pieces of yarn that are too small to knit with but too pretty to throw out, and it's so soothingly linear. Each new row builds on the one before, like in knitting or crochet, and yet it exists entirely within this predetermined space, like in embroidery. I experimented with shapes and tassels and hung the finished products in the entryway to my apartment.

And then . . . I lost interest. It wasn't the most portable craft (although at the height of my obsession I carried the loom around with me in its own tote bag) and I got a little sick of working within the same space, on something that was always the exact same size. I could have used those limitations to get creative; I could have bought a bigger loom or a smaller one, or taken a class on how to use a floor loom and made scarves and rugs and large pieces of fabric to turn into all kinds of other things.

But I didn't. I told a friend that I would make him a wall hanging more than two years ago and it's still half-done on the child-sized loom.

The real weaver, it turned out, was Moriah. She started on the same type of loom as me but figured out how to really use it, when to add one unexpected color or start an entirely new pattern out of nowhere. She did take a class; she did learn to use a floor loom; she did make scarves, even made one for me. Later, she'd use that same motion—the in and out and around of it—to make the baskets.

It wasn't her first craft—she'd been right next to me throughout my entire childhood of making things, through jewelry-making lessons with our aunt Kathleen and selling clay creations to our neighbors. Moriah quietly drew and pasted and stitched, and by the time she got to high school, she was a bona fide Art Kid, taking AP-level art classes and researching architecture programs for college. I don't think she wanted to be an architect per se, but like our mother she had always loved spaces, the way different elements fit together in real time.

When we were growing up, the two of us used to play The Sims on the family computer for hours, creating entire mundane worlds with our characters until our mother would tell us to go to bed. I had no patience for building the homes these little avatars were supposed to live in—if left to my own devices, I'd plop a bunch of furniture down in a gigantic square of walls and call it a day—but Moriah loved it. She'd add staircases and sloped ceilings, would take five minutes to select the wallpaper for a room, and when she was done I would reclaim the mouse and get down to the real business of the game: forcing my Sims to make out and then killing them. (I belong in jail.) I constructed elaborate backstories, even re-created people I knew in real life, usually boys I had crushes on. Moriah never seemed to mind, happy to watch her space being put to use. Even then, she was the artist, and I was the writer.

When Matthew came along, he completed the trifecta as the musician. Of course we didn't know that right away, but it didn't take long; by the time he was eight he had started guitar lessons, and by eleven or twelve it was clear that here was a kid with real talent. Now he plays everything: drums, guitar, viola, alto sax, piano. He can pick up anything you put in front of him, and teaches kids throughout the summer and school year. The writer, the artist, and the musician, born to two people who met at an accounting firm: I've always loved the mythology of us, the way the story sounds.

And the story of me and Moriah goes that I claimed her right away.

"You can call her Charlotte if you want to," I'm told I said at age three, as my parents deliberated over possible names for the forthcoming baby, "but since I'm going to call her Moriah, she might get confused."

Another quote I was too young to remember saying: "She's going to be my best friend."

There are other snippets: for years, my favorite outfit was a green dress my bubbe, my father's mother, had given me, because Moriah had a matching one. I brought Moriah into show-and-tell at kindergarten. We ran our lemonade-and-clay stands and sold everything at an egregious markup. I cut her hair, and I stuck gift bows to her head, and once, when we got a red wagon for Hanukkah, I put her in it and wheeled her down the street, trying to give her away. Not because I wanted to get rid of her—just the opposite. I loved this smiley little person so much that all I wanted was to share her with the rest of the world.

I don't know which of these things really happened, apart from a few corroborating photos: us in our matching dresses, us brandishing boxes of clay things, Moriah with three shiny bows affixed to her hair. But I like the comfort in stories, their defined beginnings and ends. Nothing ragged or circuitous, nothing I can't make sense of.

I would like this to be a story of how crafting saved my sister. On some level, that might be true; on another, it's far too neat. And it's still ongoing, so it's hardly a story at all, just a series of sometimes-connected-sometimes-not things that happened.

Moriah got into architecture school, a great one, and left home for St. Louis. The beginning seemed all right, but as time went on she started to call our mother in the middle of the night, breathless with tears. Moriah eventually transferred from the architecture program to art, where she made collages and large-scale prints of monsters and pieced together found objects from Goodwill. My mother's calls to me got more and more worried—she was fielding Moriah's calls at increasingly odd hours, even flew out to St. Louis a few times to be with her. Moriah mostly stopped responding to my texts, which were usually just clunky messages asking if she was okay interspersed with animal memes I found on the Internet. No one could decide if college was the right place for her to be, if the structure it provided was supporting or suffocating her. She couldn't always finish her work, couldn't always get out of bed, couldn't always name what was happening to her. She became sadder and more manic by turns, and none of us knew what to do.

In the small, white, wealthy town where we grew up, there

was a way that you did things. Even when I was young I heard families talking about how they "moved here for the school system," and that system had a purpose: to get you into college. Homework, rehearsals, SAT prep, guidance counselors all pitched in to get us to this seemingly final destination. We didn't really talk about what happened once you arrived, and there was no map if you thought you might want to go someplace else.

When it got to be too much, Moriah left school and came home.

Somewhere in there she spent time in an inpatient program. It was Shark Week; she told me later that she remembered because it was all they were allowed to watch, and because a boy said that he had been there that time last year too. That made her sad. It also made her sad that they weren't allowed scissors or other "sharps," and so she had to make collages by ripping up pieces of paper. Even though she'd been in school to make collages and prints and all kinds of things, and the scissors were never the problem.

Things got worse, and better, and back again. She went on an architecture trip to Germany that she had to come home early from, and a crafting trip to a school in Maine where she managed to stay the whole time. That was where she learned to sew rope and make baskets; after two weeks she'd made enough to cover the branches of a tree. The baskets looked like beehives or naturally occurring bird feeders, like they were alive or had been, like they were dripping.

She stayed at home for a while and made more baskets. She

took over the table in the sunroom and the unused nook in the hallway between our bedrooms. She took over my bedroom too, which I'd watched gradually happen each time I came home on breaks from college. I'd climb the stairs to the room and the bed would be conspicuously rumpled, a few stray articles of clothing on the armchair and unfamiliar makeup on the bureau. I think she liked how monastic it felt; she treated her own room more like a very large and well-lit closet, with piles of clothes spilling onto the floor and the coatrack and the bright-blue chaise longue. On a few visits home I slept in her bed. I didn't mind—I'd never really liked my own room, which she and I had shared when we were younger but which I'd inherited as we grew up—and I was there so infrequently that it didn't so much matter where I dropped my bag. And part of me secretly liked being in this warm and eclectic-if-messy space Moriah had created while I wasn't looking, even if I had to step over a mountain of Urban Outfitters crop tops to get there. She'd felt far away from me for a long time, and it helped remind me of who she really was.

A lot of that is secondhand. I missed so much. I was away, I was wrapped up in my own life: school, then graduating, then finding a job and finding an apartment and finding a boyfriend, and then another apartment and no boyfriend and still the same job. News of Moriah came in spurts, usually through my mom on one of our many phone calls. Moriah herself was not super open when it came to her feelings, sometimes replying when I texted her, sometimes not.

You grow up thinking that somebody who loves you should automatically know how to care for you, and vice versa. That to love is to understand, and to understand is to know exactly how to act. But so much gets lost between people. We don't even know how best to care for ourselves a lot of the time, so how could we expect to do it so effortlessly for others? I thought that if I truly loved Moriah, the way I knew I did, I should be able to help her. I should be able to give her exactly what she needed even if she didn't know it yet: analysis, clarity, a plan of action. I should be able to follow the thread back to the moment it got tangled, the instant she first slipped into this sadness, and help her unknot it. That was what I was best at; that was all that I knew how to do.

During the worst of this I would get so frustrated, at myself and at our parents and at her. Even though I knew the answer—namely, that we were different people with different chemical makeups—I could never quite understand why she couldn't push through. Why couldn't she just open her laptop, finish her finals, put her feet on the floor, and leave the room? Why couldn't the motions of productivity save her the way they had saved me, over and over again, from my anxiety and my fear and my grief?

I was frustrated when we talked about Moriah like she was a problem to be solved, and because I was the number-one perpetrator of that fantasy. I was frustrated by the barbed little remarks she'd make when I was back home—my jacket was weird, the way I made avocado toast was substandard—and how it was impossible to separate my run-of-the-mill sisterly feelings toward her from my feelings toward what she was going through. I was frustrated when our parents acted like she was made of glass and took her side because it was easier than letting her fall apart. I was frustrated because I knew she was tougher than that, if we'd just let her be.

I was frustrated with myself for being frustrated! And my frustration—which was really just helplessness in an uglier outfit—would come out as shortness, as sharpness, as slammed cups at the table and joyless laughs issued from between my teeth. It caused me to pick fights over minuscule things I should have just let lie and mutter unkind words about the person I loved best in the world, half hoping she could hear them. It made me want to kick Moriah out of the cockpit of her own brain and take over the controls myself, because of course I, above anyone else in the world (including Moriah herself), could save her.

"I need you to be my sister," she told me once on a visit to New York, when I was trying to give her advice or prescribe a course of action or doing something other than what I should have been doing, which was listening. "Not my teacher, and not my therapist."

I shut up, and we finished our breakfast in not-uneasy quiet.

Moriah went back to school after a few semesters at home; when I go back now, I sleep in my own bed again. She lived in an apartment off campus, where in typical form our mother painted the walls even though the lease was just for the year. She brought one of our family's several cats—Harry, who had belonged to our grandparents when they died. She sent us pictures of him lurking in the space between the fridge and the ceiling, or pacing around the craft corner she set up with her sewing machine and scraps and strings. And finally, after years of stopping and starting, she graduated. We all flew out to St. Louis and sobbed freely when she walked down the aisle with her classmates, when the professor handing out diplomas called her name, when she won an award signifying her work in sculpture. It's not that everything is fixed, or ever will be. It's just that it was time to keep going.

On the rare occasions when we are in the same place at the same time, I like to watch her work. Her projects are so different from anything I make, but in some ways they're the same—starting from what looks like nothing and incorporating new nothings over and over until they become a something. Her crafts are hard where mine are soft, sturdy where mine tend to flop and fold and lie flat. I like how they look next to each other: a basket of hers hangs on a doorknob in my apartment, facing the wall of embroideries and the two tiny wall hangings I made before losing interest in weaving; another sits on my bookshelf beside a pile of notebooks I've filled with scribbles, my attempts to turn my own messy life into a series of neat stories.

I have this fantasy of the two of us opening a store together where we sell our stuff, a sort of general-store-meets-yarn-store-meets-coffee-shop (-meets-bar, knowing us). Moriah snorts at me when I get too sentimental, when I get too ahead of myself or gush about being proud of how far she's come; she knows, better than I do, that this is not over, that there is so much further for all of us to go. But I don't mind being the sentimental sister, the lover of neatness and narratives, one of a pair of crafters. In fact, it sounds like a pretty good story.

The Weather Was Better
Before You Woke Up

To my knowledge, my dad has never made a hat. He doesn't knit or crochet, doesn't sew or embroider. I can hardly even remember seeing him draw a picture. When he sits in silence, in his favorite armchair in Boston or at the dining-room table in Rhode Island, it's usually with an iPad in hand, or a sheaf of work papers. Not like me, with my hands that are never still, always fluttering to bring small things into the world. But the older I get, the more I realize that we are made of the same stuff.

In Rhode Island, he wakes up before dawn. He tries to be quiet, to collect his boots and fishing pole without rousing the rest of us, but the walls in the house by the beach are thin. Doors stick or else burst open without much more provocation than a breeze; floors creak like stifled laughter.

He rustles and putters and is out the door before the sun is a sliver. Sometimes our dog joins in, although the only help he offers is company and a permanent smile. Sometimes my dad drags a kayak down to the ocean or the nearby breachway (a word I learned from him) and paddles out to meet the fish. Usually, though, he stands on the shore and he waits.

I do not do the pre-sunrise ritual but I often stir when he does, and even though I exaggerate my yawns later in the day, I'm glad for it. I like to lie in the twin bed I take when I visit and watch the sky streaks through the window. I like to doze off and wake up again for a minute when he comes back home, dumps his gear in the garage, and puts on a pot of coffee that's still hot three hours later when the rest of us are alive. I like to bear out-of-sight witness to this ritual my father has built for himself over the past few years. He's extended the invitation for Moriah and Matthew and me to join him, but we are the type to sleep until ten and make a lot of noise. We are not the type, as our dad is now, to let fish or tides tell us what to do.

"Too bad you slept so long," he'll say, even if we do happen to be awake at eight, even if the sky is perfectly blue and the air is just the right level of warm. "It was even nicer out there this morning." We roll our eyes and drink all of the remaining coffee.

My dad worked hard when I was growing up, and still does. He's been at the same accounting firm since he graduated college, moving his way up to partner, spending late nights and early mornings at the office and traveling everywhere from Dublin to Midland, Michigan, to see his various clients. Our relationship is quieter than the one I have with my mom, fewer phone calls about boys and more emails about tax returns. But as close as my mom and I are, my dad is the person I really take after (and not just in the nose and eyebrows department). He is sociable and straightforward, like me; sarcastic and impatient, like me; likes to fix things, like me; and to know that everyone he loves will be okay, will be provided for, will be safe. Every day he's worked has been in the service of making sure we are happy. And when he needs to field the odd boy-related phone call, he always comes through.

Following his example, I worked hard too. I got straight A's and performed in musicals and quit softball as soon as it started interfering with choir practice. I wasn't unhappy in high school—I had my series of boyfriends, my small but strong group of friends-friends, and I actually kind of enjoyed doing homework—and I loved the comforts and rhythms of my family, but I couldn't wait to get out of our suburb and head to college. Once I did, I only dipped back home a couple of times a year for breaks. I didn't see exactly when the subtle yet strong transformation in my dad took hold.

What I do know is that one summer my folks, seemingly out of the blue, rented a small house near the beach in Rhode Island, about an hour away from where they still lived, in Boston.

"Wait, *what's* the town called?" I asked, three or four times.

"Quonochontaug," they would reply. "But you can just call it Quonnie."

So I did. Quonnie turned out to be the site of what I less-than-half-jokingly describe as the gentlest midlife crisis in history, the moment my dad slowed down and looked inward. And it was all, seemingly, because of fishing.

He had golfed on and off through most of my life and so was no stranger to early alarms and long, dragged-out spells of silent concentration bundled up as communal male sport, but fishing was different. It came with no handicap. It didn't require acres of land or a group of three other accountants; it didn't require permission or planning or witness at all, except for when the dog went along. It meant he had new gear to research, new permits to acquire, new modes of transportation to buy (he owns, for some reason, two kayaks, even though he has only one body). He learned about lures and bait, how to read tides and tie knots. He had the thing that I've sought, in some way or another, for my whole life: a series of soothing, repeatable tasks.

Eventually my dad found his fishing companion, a man named (honest-to-God) Gil, who is twenty years his senior, and they would go out in the mornings together. Where other fishermen would jealously guard their best spots, Gil and my dad would share; after an especially great solo outing, my dad would call Gil like a preteen with juicy gossip to spill. He grew a beard, which he kept, and a little bit of a belly, which he tried to vanquish. He slowed down, worked from home a few days a week, wore his life much more comfortably. He seemed, for the first time in my life, like he'd found peace.

Before I left school, my parents bought the house next door to the place they had rented. Even though it was a new load for him to bear, this mortgage that meant my dad had to continue working as hard as ever, he never regretted it. The house meant that he could wake up and be on the water within minutes. It meant there was a space for all of us to gather that wasn't quite home and wasn't our respective other places—school, work— with their accompanying responsibilities and stresses.

At first I was unconvinced. "You replaced me with a *house*?" I'd say. I spent my own summers working at camp and then in New York, feeling happy and lucky to go down to the beach for a week but never really understanding the draw of the place. Much like in Delaware before, some obnoxious little voice in me kept asking why anyone had elected to put a beach in Rhode Island.

"Is it near Providence?" a friend would ask.

"Yes."

"How about Newport?"

"Yep."

It's near everything because everywhere in Rhode Island, the most diminutive state in this great nation, is near everything. Quonnie (technically not a town but a "fire district") is tiny and nearby Westerly is too, with a few restaurants and bars and one really excellent coffee shop/clothing store. There used to be a yarn store, which closed, but now there is one of those cavernous, suburban-style Michaels. There is also, miraculously, an Amtrak station.

This turned out to make all the difference for me. I discovered that I could hop on a train out of Penn Station and be at my parents' doorstep in a little over three hours. I could escape the smells and the heat of the city baking itself in the dead of summer. I could avoid, at least for a weekend, the boring yet deeply demanding litany of *needs* that make up my everyday life, and settle back into the nest of my family (which has its own needs, of course, but at least they're different from the usual menu). It was so liberating to realize that what feels like the impossibly strong gravitational pull of my city and my job and my sense of who I have to be isn't actually that hard to resist. My dad feels the same way; for all that my mom loves the house, which she appointed with her characteristically warm touch, and Moriah and Matthew like the beach and the infinite supply of beer, it's my dad and I who look forward to summers the most, who talk about it obsessively on the family group text in between pictures of the now-four pets. We like the salty smell and the soft light. We like our lower frequencies, our calmer minds. We like who we are there.

It's not like Boston is that much farther from New York—maybe an hour and a half longer by train—but I've never had quite the same urge to go home-home as I do to visit Rhode

Island. Home-home is where the nest can quickly become a black hole, sucking me into the same spot on the couch and back into the same person I used to be when I was fourteen. I don't love who I am there; I'm cranky and bratty, all of a sudden incapable of putting my dishes in the sink and prone to staying up until the birds start to chirp, doing next to nothing. It feels a little too heavy, a little too layered, a little more like regressing than revisiting.

But going to Rhode Island is clean. It's light. I bring almost nothing—there are toothbrushes and pajamas there already—and exhale more fully. It does mean contending with Penn Station, which if you have never visited is like if a midsize strip mall were located inside an armpit, and Amtrak tickets can cost as much as a trip aboard a vehicle that's actually capable of flight; similarly, my dad has to battle traffic and tolls and poisonously early alarms in order to make it back and forth as often as he does. We both know, though, that it's never once not been worth it.

Fishing, I believe, is my dad's version of crafting, a place where he can focus on his breath and the patterns that he and the waves have worked out together. He knows how to read the tides and the weather the way I can read a piece of knitted fabric or Moriah can read a basket, and decide how to proceed from there. We all get to be experts. We all get to give ourselves over to things that are at once much bigger and much smaller than we are. Did you know that your parents are also people? I didn't.

"Look what I made!" I crow when I've finished the last row on a hat or a scarf. After twenty years of crafting you'd think it would get old. Maybe it has for the people I'm yelling to, but for me, never.

"Caught a keeper today," my dad says as soon as one of us stumbles bleary-eyed down the stairs in the morning. It doesn't always happen—many days he doesn't get a bite, and when he does, if it's under twenty-eight inches or will just go to waste, he throws the fish back anyway—but when conditions are aligned, we wake up to a freezer full of striped bass. And honestly it doesn't seem to matter if he catches something or not; he always comes back calmer and happier than when he left, not like in the days of golf, with its scorekeeping and wins and losses.

On the days when he does catch something, though, he and my mom will turn it into fish tacos, and the five of us will crowd around the table on the back porch and gamely eat the product of my dad's labor, his hobby, his love.

I wake up. Not as early as the first shift, but before my dad is done with his post-fishing nap. I patter down the creaky wooden stairs, past Matthew snoozing facedown on the couch (he has a bed but seems to prefer this option), past the begging eyes of the dog, left behind this time. I pour myself a mug of coffee and slip out the back door and head toward the beach. Even in summer it's fairly empty at this hour—the fishermen have mostly packed away their things and the beachgoers haven't yet arrived to stake out their spots—and in the fall and early spring it will be downright deserted. You can stare down the coast for miles and not see another person.

I like to sit on this one benchlike piece of driftwood when the tide is in, and atop a smooth collection of rocks when it's out. Sometimes I bring my knitting but mostly I just sit, kicking off my sandals, breathing in the salt air before the day and the caffeine kick in. From here I feel like I can see forever: my future kids, rolling around in the sand with their cousins, getting so tired they almost fall asleep on the short walk back to their grandparents' house. (Which by then will have an entire insulated wing so my parents can stay there year-round—even now it's open from basically March until Thanksgiving, daring the pipes to freeze.) Maybe one of them will take an interest in fishing; like knitting, I've heard it skips a generation.

There are so many ifs—if I find someone I want to reproduce with who wants that as well, if I can have kids, if the same goes for my siblings, if climate change doesn't gobble up the shoreline and all the surrounding real estate. If we all still like one another. If we're all still here to see it.

But on the beach in the morning, the ifs feel very far away. I stay for maybe fifteen or twenty minutes before returning home, shoes still in hand. My dad is awake by now, rinsing out the coffee pot and preparing more for the rest of the family.

"How is it out there?" he asks.

"Beautiful," I say. "But probably not as nice as this morning."

Casting Off

I've been working on a blanket for years. This is unusual for me. I tend to plow through projects in concentrated bursts, a month or two at most. If I can't seem to make the *Flashdance*-inspired sweater or the ill-advised pair of knee socks work, I eventually unravel them and put the yarn toward some other use. I have my small pile of perpetually unfinished objects (UFOs) but their fate is uncertain; chances are, there's a reason I've tossed them into the basket at the foot of my bed, and it's not because I plan on falling in love with them one of these days. Maybe the fit wasn't right or the pattern was too hard to understand. Maybe I ran out of the color of yarn I wanted, or decided I didn't actually need a set of crocheted succulent planters when I already own a set of non-crocheted succulent planters. Maybe—most likely—it was because I lost momentum, or because my desire to be done grew so strong that it latched itself onto the next project, and the next and the next, leaving these little not-quite-rights behind to be eventually, inevitably discarded.

But my unfinished blanket will one day be done. I know this the way that I know the sun will come up tomorrow. For one thing, I've already invested enough time and money in it that there's no turning back now, and for another, I want it very badly. And for another-nother, I want to prove to myself that I can really do it. My friend Anne ran the New York City Marathon; she trained all year. Aude and I went and stood along the route in Brooklyn and then took the subway to the finish line in Manhattan. We complained about the cold and our aching feet the entire time, even though we were not the people responsible for running 26.2 miles.

This blanket is my little marathon—a half, maybe. Not something that can be completed in a week or even a month, something that feels insurmountable if you try to envision the whole thing at once but that can be accomplished bit by tiny bit. Plus, I get to sit on the couch while I work on it.

I was always a little surprised when I'd remember that I hadn't made a blanket before, beyond those first stabs at doll-sized home decor. I'd made everything else that I could think of, often just to figure out how a thing was constructed, or to prove that I could: a reusable market bag for the grocery store, a floor pouf stuffed with towels that's so heavy I can't lift it with one hand, a saggy off-white bikini top that makes my boobs look like day-old pancakes. The allure of these experiments was in the process, and in the taming of an everyday object—oh, so *that's* how you seam up something that weighs as much as a medium-sized dog; *that's* how you shape fabric intended to house a round rather than a tubular part of the body. I hold on to these projects not because I need yet another eco-friendly method of carrying tomatoes in the tote bag capital of America, but because they're physical reminders of problems I've solved, techniques I've mastered.

So, then, a blanket: at its heart it's the most elemental item you can make. Just endless rows, back and forth, ad infinitum. Shouldn't that be no problem after hours spent figuring out wrap-and-turns and three-needle bind-offs? And hadn't afghans been my grandma's bread and butter, my earliest example of what someone armed with a crochet hook and a pile of yarn could do? I'd grown up surrounded by homemade blankets—my bubbe (my father's mother) made them too, knitted our family a beautiful throw that was lined with red and gold fabric on one side. This might have meant that I didn't feel the need to add another to the pile, but that had never stopped me from making more scarves, sweaters, and socks than a single reasonable person could ever wear in a lifetime.

Maybe part of my blanket aversion had to do with the simplicity, that omnipresence—a blanket didn't seem like a worthy challenge. Sure, it would take approximately forever, but there were no interesting problems to be solved in stitching row after row. Besides, you can't wear a blanket out in public and smile benignly at cries of "You *made* that?!" A blanket has to live in one place.

Don't get me wrong, I've always been a lover of blankets. All three of us kids had special ones. Mine was pink and patterned with sheep on one side (I like to think it was a harbinger of the many thousands of dollars I would grow up to spend on wool) and quilted in white on the other. It was the kind of soft that sticks to your skin even after you're done touching it.

I called it my blankie and carried it around everywhere, along with an old stuffed lion named Gloria. Gloria used to belong to my mother and weighed about eight pounds, which made sense when I accidentally (I think) sliced open her tail one day and found that she was full not of stuffing but of hard white beads. I have a distinct memory of sneaking Gloria into my bubbe's pool. She sank.

My blankie, though, was sacred. I liked to snuggle under it and wear it as a cape and use it as a cornerstone in my many forts—my favorite method was to unzip the cover of my comforter and nestle inside, cuddled up with my blankie and maybe a book in this dreamy, warm space. Even before I knew anything about fabric or yarn, I liked to create these tiny worlds to my exact specifications.

And my pursuit of cozy has never been anything compared

to Moriah's. It's practically her catchphrase: the shriek of "Cozy!!!!" accompanied by a dive for the squashiest couch cushion or the pile of fresh-from-the-dryer bed linens. Her cozy drive is as strong as a truffle dog's, pointing her in the direction of oversize sweaters and elastic-waist pants that are somehow cuter than anything I've ever been able to pull off, plus a formidable array of Snuggies. Moriah collapses into her soft, safe spaces with an exhalation that sounds like nothing so much as relief.

Her childhood blanket was woven, made up of thousands of pastel threads that grew flimsier with each wash. When she got older, Matthew inherited it, in the classic tradition of third children everywhere. But he managed to make it his own. He christened it his "may-may" and put my blankie commitment to shame, taking it really, truly, appallingly everywhere. You could tell where it had been because it started to disintegrate, leaving a few trailing threads ("may-may strings") in its wake. Once, our family went on a trip to Puerto Rico and slept on a sailboat, and when I looked out at the sea the next morning I saw a cluster of may-may strings caught on a piece of rock, fluttering in the salty breeze.

When his may-may became little more than a shred, Matthew transferred his affections. He adopted a beautiful, understated throw from Restoration Hardware that our mother had intended for use in the living room, and spent his remaining blankie-loving days carrying it around. He's outgrown it now but when I picture his bedroom I still superimpose on it that lovely, muted blanket, totally at odds with his Pokémon-patterned sheets.

Those pieces of fabric were as much a part of us, for a time, as our hairstyles or our sandals. They meant we were protected, that even if things on the outside were scary or overwhelming we could still envelop ourselves, could block out the sound and the light. Where does that impulse go once you've outgrown its container? Into relationships, into apartments, into a ceaseless march of craft projects?

I decided to make my blanket in my old apartment, in my old relationship, right as I was beginning to strain at the edges of both. I spent hours fantasizing about what a solid, solo life could look like and always came back to this hazy idea of warmth, of hunkering down and pulling the corners around me tight, needing and wanting nothing other than what I could give myself. Making a blanket seemed like the most literal possible embodiment of that vision.

I bought cheap yarn since I knew I'd need a lot of it, more than I'd ever needed for a single project before. I chose a soft cotton in cream and deep pink and navy blue. A craft blog I followed had instructions simple enough for even my junior-varsity crochet skills. I was to start with a circle of six stitches—about the diameter of a nickel—and work outward, making what's known as a granny square. Even non-crocheters will recognize granny squares: picture a blanket on a great-aunt's couch or a vest worn by an especially zany art teacher. Chances are, it's made of dozens of little multicolored squares all sewn together. They're recognizable by how they sort of explode out from the center, a blue circle inside a yellow one inside a white square. Like an optical illusion with no illusion. Alone they make good coasters or washcloths, and together they form objects that are larger and more complicated than the sum of their parts.

But my blanket would just be one granny square. A gigantic one, building row by row into a square large enough to cover my double bed, and then some. This pattern subverted the usual way of doing things by boiling it down to its simplest component. Every row would be slightly longer than the one that came before; I'd switch colors every two rows so that it wouldn't get too boring. I would stop only once I had run out of yarn, and maybe not even then.

At first, I treated the blanket like any other project. I carried it around in my bag and worked on it whenever I had a spare moment. But within a few weeks it required its own separate tote, and then after a few more it was too big to bring outside the house. It was like Alice (of Wonderland fame) after she scarfs down the "Eat Me" cakes, her legs sticking out of the windows and her neck out of the chimney. I'd never before worked on a long-term project that wasn't portable; occasionally sweaters become too heavy and floppy in their final stages as they wait for a sleeve cuff or a hem, but they're still no more of a pain to lug around than, you know, a sweater.

Because of its size, I'm forced to sit with it. I can really only work on it in one place, the couch, unless I want to drag it over to my bed. It lives in one spot and I come to it, instead of the other way around. It already looks like it belongs there, permanently draped over the arm nearest the window; if you don't lift it up to reveal the gigantic ball of yarn and the crochet hook hanging off it, it looks like any other blanket. In fact, it *acts* like any other blanket; just because it's unfinished doesn't mean it can't keep me warm while I work on it, my legs tucked underneath. Visitors to my house have complimented me on it, asked me if I made it, to which I reply, "Yes. I mean, I'm *making* it."

I crochet it occasionally, haltingly, when the mood strikes. I go months without touching it, and then there are weeks when I work on it every night when I get home. For a while I did it first thing in the morning, just a couple of stitches at a time, because I liked how large and grounding it felt as I stared down the rest of my day. It's a metaphor, sure, but it also just *is*. That's something I've always loved about crafts: they can contain so much meaning, stand for so much more than they are, and still just be exactly their own size and shape.

I did move the blanket from its place on my couch, once. The Christmas right after my grandpa died and right before my grandma did, I brought it with me to Virginia. It was enormous at that point and thus required its own piece of carry-on luggage (they tried to make me "stow it planeside" on the second leg of the journey, which takes place in an airborne tin can that seats about twenty people, but I refused). I kept the bag at my feet, leaning down to pat it a few times like it was a terrified cat in a carrier.

I flew on Christmas Day because it was cheaper and because that year felt different anyway. JFK was quiet. I loved it—the five-minute wait in the security line, the breakfast pizza (!) and Bloody Mary I ordered from a strange robotic iPad server in the middle of the terminal, how everyone, staff and fellow travelers alike, was extremely nice, almost conspiratorial, all of us stuck together in this in-between space.

When I arrived in Roanoke, it felt like I had landed in a museum. It's a tiny airport, with only a couple of gates and two runways. Security only ever takes five minutes, and there is now a single bar, which serves a Bloody Mary prepared and delivered to you by a living, breathing person. You can see from one end of the long hallway down to where your welcoming committee waits to greet you—your parents smiling and waving, your siblings off at the gift shop, your aunt with her camera, your grandfather tall and solid, your grandma ready to wrap you in her arms and comment on your hair color.

But that day there was no one. I went down the escalator and out to the parking lot. Virginia is always warmer than New York and that Christmas was balmy, too warm for the knitted presents I had in my non-blanket-containing carry-on. My mother pulled up in her parents' car and drove me back through the mountains to Blacksburg, where the tree was still waiting to be decorated and the Christmas movies were still waiting to be watched.

"Why don't we just have Christmas tomorrow?" someone suggested, and we were all grateful. We used to make fun of a family in our old neighborhood, who on one rainy Halloween called the other parents and tried to move trick-or-treating to the next night. You couldn't move a holiday, we scoffed, the same way you couldn't move an ocean. Besides, we knew how to deal with the rain: wrap your whole self in a windbreaker, or for bonus points incorporate it into your costume, and there's that much more candy for you, the most intrepid trick-or-treater of all.

But sometimes, it turns out, you do need to rearrange. You have to account for the fact that there isn't a large, thoughtful presence anchoring the head of the kitchen table any longer. You have to be slower, to understand your own limits. You have to make new traditions.

"Look," I said to my grandma the following afternoon, on what we had now decided was Christmas. "Look what I'm making."

"Oh, that's lovely," she said, touching the familiar-to-her rows of double-crochet.

It's all because of you, I thought but didn't say, because I guess I thought I'd have forever. *All of it.*

The following winter, after my grandma had died too, we held Christmas at our house in Needham. We'd never even had a tree of our own before, and thus had no ornaments or lights or backlog of history to draw from. We gave only the gifts that were wanted, instead of the usual mountain: I got a kettle and an electric toothbrush, Moriah got clothes and boots, Matthew got socks. Without my grandma and grandpa it felt a little hollow, a touch perfunctory, as if we were going through the motions because we didn't know what else to do. We were all tense; I picked a couple of fights. But there were glimmers of new rituals. Moriah made ornaments out of wicker and wood; the following year, the two of us made stockings for everyone, even the pets.

When I started my blanket, I didn't know who I would be dating when it was finished. I didn't know where I would live, or what my job would be, or which of my friends and family would still be around. I didn't even know if I'd still want it! It's a leap of faith, making something so large. You have to believe that you'll still feel the same pull that started you off in the first place, even if you don't know where it will go or who you will be. Even if you still don't once it's finished.

The rows are so long now. Each side measures at least five feet; it's rare that I finish a full round in a single sitting. And the size makes it almost impossible to determine progress. Increasing by two stitches every row means a lot when there are only twelve or sixteen stitches total, but practically nothing when there are hundreds. How are you supposed to know when you've made an impact, gotten further, are closer to where you finally want to end up?

What I've realized is that you can't, at least not moment to moment. When you zoom out, you'll see what you've done—you can wrap yourself in it, feel the weight of it, even if it seems at the time like it's made of thousands of nothings. All you can do is trust what you do know, what years of making things and fucking up and starting over have taught you. Each stitch is a step forward, even if you're going in circles. (Or squares.) Each minute was well spent. Look at that: you made it.

ACKNOWLEDGMENTS

The greatest thanks my yarn-loving heart can muster go to Kate McKean, an incomparable agent and sounding board and knitting buddy and friend.

To Amy Einhorn, whose belief in this project and whose guidance, patience, edits, and general brilliance shaped it into something so much more than the swirling threads of thoughts in my own brain; and to Conor Mintzer, Caroline Bleeke, Kimberly Escobar, Molly Fonseca, and the whole Flatiron team who helped get it out into the world.

To my earliest readers and editors, who made me feel like this was something worthwhile even when I didn't know what it would or could look like: Anne Speyer, Liz Kossnar, Arianna Rebolini, Katie Heaney, Rachel Sanders, Rachel Miller, Jen Doll, Doree Shafrir, Mark Schoofs, and Isaac Fitzgerald; and to my old BuzzFeed family and my new Racked one.

To the Millettes, who so generously opened their home to me, where I wrote more words, drank more coffee, and knitted more socks than pretty much the rest of my life combined.

To Leela, Chris, and Violet, who have been the greatest "landfamily" a transplant New Yorker could ever hope for.

To Amitava Kumar and Dean Crawford, who I will probably be hounding for advice and recommendation letters long after the Vassar school song has faded from my memory.

To the Night Owls and the Young New Yorkers' Chorus, who helped me find my voice; and to the Charles River Creative Arts Program, the first place where I learned the value of making things; and to the Thread, which has always felt like home.

To my family, the reason for it all.

And to Aude White, whose friendship sustains me and makes me better, and to Brendan Klinkenberg, the best wearer of sweaters I know.

Recommend *The Curse of the Boyfriend Sweater*
for your next book club!
Reading Group Guide available at
www.readinggroupgold.com